Alien Abductions

Alien Contact In The Form Of Human Abductions

(True Stories Of Ufo Sightings And Alien Abductions)

Robert Shields

Published By **Ryan Princeton**

Robert Shields

All Rights Reserved

Alien Abductions: Alien Contact In The Form Of Human Abductions(True Stories Of Ufo Sightings And Alien Abductions)

ISBN 978-1-77485-598-0

No part of this guidebook shall be reproduced in any form without permission in writing from the publisher except in the case of brief quotations embodied in critical articles or reviews.

Legal & Disclaimer

The information contained in this ebook is not designed to replace or take the place of any form of medicine or professional medical advice. The information in this ebook has been provided for educational & entertainment purposes only.

The information contained in this book has been compiled from sources deemed reliable, and it is accurate to the best of the Author's knowledge; however, the Author cannot guarantee its accuracy and validity and cannot be held liable for any errors or omissions. Changes are periodically made to this book. You must consult your doctor or get professional medical advice before using any of the suggested remedies, techniques, or information in this book.

Upon using the information contained in this book, you agree to hold harmless the Author from and against any damages, costs, and expenses, including any legal fees potentially resulting from the application of any

Table of contents

Introduction

The Importance of Alien Abduction How to Know If You've Been Kidnapped and Learn the Stories of Those who have. Apart from being familiar with abductions by aliens and alien abductions, you'll be able to tell whether or not you've been taken by aliens in the past and learn about the experiences of people who were taken hostage by paranormal forces.

In the course of time, a series of movies like Communion, E.T., Night Skies, Taken, and The Fourth Kind may have at least sparked your interest about aliens and abductions by aliens. If you've had an experience that you think you've been taken to a location that you aren't able to identify It's impossible to affirm that you didn't get abducted. Particularly since numerous accounts of this sort of the abductions from around the globe have been reported that you should investigate the real situation.

It doesn't matter if your fascination with the subject came through exposure to the satirical films about aliens as well as

1

captivating documentaries or deeper, it's likely that you'll get to the point at which you feel the desire to find the bottom of the matter. Did you get abducted? Or not? Maybe it's time to clarify some ideas. If you're unsure of the subject of alien abductions, you'll get your head straight after you start reading this book.

Enjoy!

Chapter 1: How It All Started

There are proof of encounters with aliens and alien abductions that date to hundreds of years ago, however, if you were to determine the beginning date of the modern-day alien abductions, then you'd need to begin with an incident like Betty as well as Barney Hill. This incident is well-known to everyone with even the slightest curiosity about UFOs as well as Aliens. A specially-made TV film was made starring James Earl Jones as Barney Hill and the State of New Hampshire even built a memorial to the public at the place as seen in the following photo:

It took place in a region known as Indian Head, New Hampshire It is widely regarded as the site of the first documented encounter between aliens and humans. Betty Barney Hill and Barney Hill were driving home the night after their trip to Canada and returned back to the United States on the night of, and in the early morning of September 19th-20th the year 1961. During this they were shocked by a flash of lighting.

Betty Hill

Betty Hill: "As it was coming out of our highways, as we stopped. we turned around and saw a curving picture window, with an red light on both side. That's why Barney grabbed his binoculars and got off the road and attempted to determine what craft it was. He could also see an entire group of men in the window , looking at him from the side; and at that point, he felt nervous, he was under the feeling that they were trying to take him captive."

In a panic, he jumped to their vehicle and ran away from the scene. However, when they got at their home, they noticed odd scratches on the front of their vehicle as well as a mysterious chemical on Betty's gown. They could not even be sure of the length of time which had passed.

Betty Hill: "Somehow we were feeling a bit of contamination. So I told Barney"This is weird. I'm not sure what I'm talking about. We'd felt touched, in some way we'd felt attracted."

The Hill's experience caused them to seek help of a renowned psychiatrist, Dr. Benjamin Simon. The sessions with hypnotherapy showed a horror unlike any previously recorded. They were in fact so traumatizing in the sense that Betty as well as Barney were unable to hear their recordings of their own sessions until a few months afterward. The story of their experiences quickly went viral, creating an explosion of interest from the media.

Betty Hill: "Well, we got noticed almost immediately. Barney as well as me would take a trip out for have a meal and people would show up to us and request our autographs."

Betty saved the dress from her incident and later displayed it to investigators as well as reporters. A portion of the dress were pink stained. She even cut a piece of the dress stained and took the dress to a lab to be examined.

Betty Hill: "You can see the blue in this photo and this is the place where it got colored by pink-colored powdered substances. This is the area that I removed the area and sent it to a laboratory. They couldn't analyse it, and they don't know what caused that red stain."

The actual transcripts of Barney Hill

The time Betty or Barney Hill underwent hypnosis, recordings were recorded of their sessions. Some of recordings from the sessions of Barney Hill found their way to the public domain and now as the first on Kindle are transcripts [1] of a few of the sessions. The hypnotist's name is the Dr. Benjamin Simon and the sessions took place beginning on January 4th of 1964 through June 6th 1964.

Barney Hill

A transcript of some from the Barney Hill's Hypnosis Sessions:

Hypnotists: Get deeper, deeper, deeper sleep. Sleep all the way. More and more deep. Completely relaxed, only relaxed, calm. You're comfortable, relaxed. You won't be stressed or stressed, but you'll keep everything in mind and be able to tell me everything.

Barney Hill: Yes. I'm thinking that I'll stop, I'll stop, but I haven't yet stopped. Betty told me, 'look! There's an eagle moving'. Then I looked up and see an eagle. Strange, but I told"Betty, it's the satellite. It's the satellite. Then I pulled up towards on the other side, and Betty was jumping out of her side, onto her side, with her binoculars. I took the chain and tied it to the dog's collar. her collar. I then told her"come here, Delsy and let's go out'. The dog jumps up and I stare at the sky. I then looked back at Delsey and then walked her through the trunk of the car, and I said"hurry up Betty so that I can take an eye.'

And Betty hands the binoculars over to me and I realize it's not a set of lights. It's actually an aircraft. It's an aircraft you can see. I believe you can see the rows of windows , and it's an aircraft. I inform Betty that and hand the binoculars to her and am pleased. When I get on the road, Betty is looking around at her, she says, "Barney this isn't an aircraft, it's in the air following us. Then I stop and look around and notice the star jutting in the distance therefore, I look for a spot to turn away from the highway.

There is an unpaved road just to the right of this main road, and I decide that it's a good spot I could get off. If a car does come to me, it will not hit me.

and I'm feeling very confused because it's still there . Betty stated that I believe she said that I'm furious at her, I told her. I think Betty attempts to convince me that it's an alien flying saucer.

Hypnotist: Was it bright enough for you to be able to be able to see?

Barney Hill: It was only a small light moving across the sky. I could hear nothing. I thought that this is absurd. And Betty this isn't an alien flying saucer, so why are you doing this to prove? You're claiming believe this phenomenon but I don't. But I don't hear any sound.

Hypnotist: Sound is not heard?

Barney Hill: I can't. I would like hearing a plane. Oh, I want to hear jets so much, I'd like to be able to listen.

Hypnotist: What makes you want to listen to a jet?

Barney Hill: Because Betty is making me mad, she's angering me. Betty is saying, "look at this, it's weird that it's not a plane take a look' I'm constantly thinking that it has to be something else - I'd like to hear an oo. I'd like to hear the sound of a motor.

Hypnotist: Just how far was it?

Barney Hill: It was not far. It was around 1,000 feet I believe.

Hypnotist One thousand feet.

Barney Hill Barney Hill: One thousand feet.

The Hypnotist: Does it move back and forth, or did it circle like an...

It's going to the west, and without being able to see, it would go straight back..if it..I envision the idea of a paddle and the ball that is made of rubber...you smash the ball, and the ball travels straight out, and then straight back with no circle. I believe it is only a jet that could fly this fast. I'm hoping that I will find a location to be able to see what it is. And I look up and see an eagle and recognize the spot I thought at first it was a wigwam. said...let's ,...in the barren house.

Hypnotist: What's this area?

Barney Hill: It is an area.

Hypnotist: What's the name of this location?

Barney Hill: It is Indian Head, I had visited before and feel at ease, but I also recognize a familiar face and I'm hoping to take a good look at this since Betty was extremely annoying She was irritated. She told me to look up and I'm unable to look at her, I'm required to drive my car, and I'm ready to get up.

Hypnotist: You're unlikely to get up as you're in a peaceful sleep and you're at ease. Relax, this isn't going to be a problem for you. Take a step forward. You'll be able to remember everything you've ever done.

Barney Hill: It's better than my left. Oh my God, what's that and how do I keep control so Betty can't tell that I'm afraid. God, I'm scared.

Hypnotist: Yes you can experience it and you can feel it, and it won't cause any harm to you.

Barney Hill: I gotta get my gun; oooh, gotta get my gun, OOOHHH!

Hypnotist: Alright, alright.

Barney Hill: I GOTTA GET MY GUN!

Hypnotist: Sleep Now take deep breaths.

(Barney begins crying and gasps)

Hypnotist: Calm down now at ease, relax. Relaxed and deep.

(Barney begins to begin to calm down.)

Hypnotist: Relaxed and calm and relaxed, you won't have to sound off. But you'll be able to be reminded of it, keep reminiscing. You're convinced that you must take out your gun, it could hurt you. You felt.

Barney Hill: I opened my trunk and I see it. I return to the car.

Hypnotist: OK, keep relatively cool.

Barney Hill: I put it in my coat, and then I take out the binoculars. It's there and I glance, and I look, and I see it's close to the ground and I'm not scared I'll take it down. I'm not worried and I take a look out, and take a walk across the street. It's up there, OH GOD DAMMIT...

Hypnotist Relax and relax It's there, you have seen it but it's not going to cause harm, so keep going.

Barney Hill: Why is it...go away...look at it...and there's a guy there.

Hypnotist: Be calm, relaxed, it's not going to harm you.

Barney Hill: And there's one man...and it's he does he have the title of captain? I'm not sure what he...it will be looking at me.

Hypnotist: Okay, take a look back a more. It's there, did you mention it was just a mile away, or a thousand yards?

Barney Hill: Oh no Barney Hill: It's not like it's that far away, it's large and not very far away. And I can tell it's moving toward me.

The Hypnotist says it tilted. what is it like now? If you say it was tilted? Did you notice windows?

Barney Hill: It looks like a large, huge pancake, with window and row of windows, and lights but there are no lights, just one massive light.

Hypnotist Window Rows like a commercial aircraft?

Barney Hill: Rows of windows, they're certainly not like commercial planes because they curve towards the sides of this pancake. I think"oh my God that's not right, I've got to stay here, this isn't real, it's not fair'. The windows are still there, and I stare at the road both ways I'm wondering if anyone can inform me that it's not there, it's not. It's the whole time...

Hypnotist: Your still asleep, but you're able to clearly see the whole thing.

Barney Hill: It's there.

Hypnotist: Are you sure that it's there?

Barney Hill: Yeah.

Hypnotist: Did you not have an epiphany?

Barney Hill: It's there.

Hypnotist: Did you get no sleep the night before?

Barney Hill: I touched my right arm, but it's not right, it's actually my left arm. I put my right arm on the table and it's my left arm. I came through.

Hypnotist: Now that you're clear You're calm.

Barney Hill: It's still there. When I allow my binoculars to fall hang from my neck, and then get them back perhaps it won't be there but it's still there. Why? What are they looking for? What are they looking for? The ,...one... is a person who is looking for me, he's smiling and he's gazing at me with his right shoulder. He's smiling, but that...

Hypnotist: Can you clearly see him?

Barney Hill: Yes, I did think

Hypnotist: What's the face like? What does it make your mind think?

Barney Hill: It's round I'm thinking of I'm thinking of a red-headed Irishman I'm not sure the reason. However, I believe I know the reason. Because Irish are generally hostile to Negroes and whenever I encounter an attractive Irish person, I respond to it by thinking that I would be at ease. And I believe this person who is looking over his shoulder friendly.

Hypnotist: When you say that you look at his shoulders, but was the man facing toward you?

Barney Hill: Yes, Barney Hill was in front of a wall.

Hypnotist: Do you remember seeing his face through the window? You claimed there were windows in a row.

Barney Hill: It was a row of windows it was a massive row of windows, but separated by...uh...struts or other structures that stopped the windows from becoming one solid window, or else it would be one large window. Then there's this ugly face on the...he appears to be the face of a German Nazi...he is an Nazi.

Hypnotist: Are you an Nazi? Did he put on an uniform?

Barney Hill: Yes

Hypnotist: What is the best uniform do you wear.

Barney Hill: It was black. He wore the black scarf that was tied around his neck and hanging on his right shoulder.

Hypnotist The Hypnotist: You pointed it out as if it were on you.

Barney Hill: I never had that thought before.

Hypnotist: A dark , tan scarf around the neck. How do you be able to see these figures so clearly from this distance?

Barney Hill: I was gazing at them through binoculars.

Hypnotist: Oh. Do they have faces that resemble others? You said one of them was reminiscent of an red-headed Irishman.

Barney Hill: His eyes were slanted. I can see it , his eyes were slanted, but not as an Chinese.

Hypnotist Who Was Betty doing all the time?

Barney Hill: I'm not close to her, so I don't know.

Hypnotist: Aren't you all alone today? You don't even think about her, and she's not speaking?

Barney Hill: I can't hear her.

Hypnotist: Did you issue any public appeal to her? What did you do to me?

Barney Hill: I,I,..I can't remember. I'm not sure I don't know.

Hypnotist: You'd recall it in the event that you had.

Barney Hill: I did not. I am aware that the creature, this leader is trying to tell me something.

Hypnotist: He's telling something. How? What is his method of getting this information?

Barney Hill: I can see it in his eyes.

Hypnotist: Can you notice his lips moving? Yes?

Barney Hill: No his lips aren't moving.

Hypnotist: Yes. He'll let you know.

Barney Hill: He's looking at me.

A Hypnotist: Tell me what he share with you?

Barney Hill: Stay there and look around, keep looking and keep looking keep looking.

Hypnotist: Can you hear his voice?

Barney Hill: ...ah I must remove these binoculars from my eyes, because if I don't , I'll continue to stare.

Hypnotist: Can you hear him say this?

Barney Hill: Ah no, he didn't say it.

Hypnotist: You thought that he was saying it.

Barney Hill: I know.

Hypnotist: He did.

Barney Hill: It's there I'm sure you'll be able to keep there and listen to what he's telling me.

Hypnotist: Alright.

Barney Hill: How'd he find my head. Don't take the binoculars off. God provide me with the strength. Take them back down. RUN! RUN! PULL THE BINOCULARS DOWN and RUN. God is a God provide me with strength, I've got to escape (hysterical)ohh, oh..you gotta get away from me..

Hypnotist: Okay I'm calm and relax.

Barney Hill: I'm dying,..I'm going to escape.

Hypnotist: Can you know if the person is telling you this? Relax, you're still in deep sleep. What can you do to be certain that he told you this?

Barney Hill: His eyes are, well, his eyes. I've never seen such eyes before.

Hypnotist: You claimed they were friendly, you claimed they were nice.

Barney Hill: Oh the Leaders, not him were not watching his back.

Hypnotist: Ah, I know the leader was the one who was the leader. How did you know that the other did not have the title of leader?

Barney Hill: Because everybody moved. Everyone was looking at me, but they all went to the leaders at the back, or moved to the large board, which appeared to be a board, but only this one , with the black, shiny jacket and scarf remained in the window. I'm driving.

Hypnotist: Do you want to go back to the car?

Barney Hill: Yes.

Hypnotist: You took the binoculars away, did you?

Barney Hill: I got em down, yes.

Hypnotist: When you got in the car, you didn't say anything to Betty.

Barney Hill: I'm getting myself in a position. I'm telling myself to hold on and don't be afraid You've got a lot of courage You can drive the car, and if you do... was said to Betty to keep her eyes open and I could see the object in the vicinity. The object was visible moving around us. I noticed it as we were passing by. The object. When I got into my vehicle, had swung around, so that it appeared to be visible. I knew it was there. It's there.. But it's not something I'm aware...funny.

Hypnotist: Yes, talk more clearly.

Barney Hill: I know the three. Oh that eye, they're in my head. Do you think I can wake up?

Hypnotist: Rest for a bit longer but we'll get through it right now. It'll pass. Your feelings will be forming will not bother you as much.

Barney Hill: Isn't that amusing? Oh, the woods.

Hypnotist Says: Yes

Barney Hill: That crazy dog. She's in the car every day. Isn't it funny. She is at the wheel.

Hypnotist: She's not barking and does nothing.

Barney Hill: She just remains there.

Hypnotist: What's with Betty?

Barney Hill: I don't know.

Hypnotist: Is shen't she saying something?

Barney Hill: No. I don't understand, are we being robbed? I...I don't know.

Hypnotist: What's it that makes you believe that you're being taken?

Barney Hill: I know what's going through my head and I'm not willing to share that.

Hypnotist: You can speak to me. you can do it right now.

Barney Hill: They're men who wear black jackets. I'm not able to pay for anything. I'm not able to find anything. I'm not sure. Oh, the eyes are there Always there. They're covering me up; I'm not worried. Are there any accidents on the road? What's the bright, bright color of the red.

Hypnotist Red? Bright?

Barney Hill: Yeah, red and orange.

Hypnotist: Where's this?

Barney Hill: Right down the road.

Hypnotist: Up the road.

Barney Hill: I don't need to be worried. But they won't speak to me.

Hypnotist: Who doesn't speak to you?

Barney Hill: The men.

Hypnotist: In the car?

Barney Hill: No, there's a road in front of you.

Hypnotist: Where are you? I'm in the vehicle?

Barney Hill: No, I'm suspended. I'm just floating around. Oh, how funny. I'm floating around. I'm desperate to get back in the car, but am I'm just floating.

Hypnotist: You're floating around or is that how you feel.

Barney Hill: The way I feel.

Hypnotist: Aren't you still outside of your vehicle?

Barney Hill: No.

Hypnotist: Are you in the car?

Barney Hill: I'm not in the car, I'm not inside the car I'm nowhere in woods. and I'm not driving.

Hypnotist: So, where are these guys?

Barney Hill: I don't know.

Hypnotist: Are you on the road?

Barney Hill: I don't know what I'm doing, I'm just floating around. The scene is ,... an absolute blast! this is the most funniest thing ever! Betty ,...funniest thing ever. I've didn't believe in flying saucers. I don't really know, not even the mysteries I'm sure I won't speak to anyone regarding this. It's ridiculous, isn't it. It's funny, I'm curious what they were thinking about when they started. Oh my god, I wish I had been there with the group...

Hypnotist: Do you wish you would have gone with them?

Barney Hill: Yes. I'd have experienced going to another planet. Perhaps this would prove that God exists. God Isn't it funny. It is possible to find evidence that of God in other worlds. Were you scared? I didn't feel scared ... actually, I was not scared. In the end, it wasn't really anything. It's absurd that I'm even talking about it. I'll be arriving in Portsmouth earlier than I had hoped.

Hypnotist: Okay, we'll end here. You'll feel calm and peaceful. You'll forget everything you've been through together , until I ask you to recall it all over again. The memory will fade of everything that we've experienced until I request you to recall it all over again. It is possible to wake up today.

Wow! It's been two minutes since eight. Didn't you bring me in here ten minutes after eight?

Hypnotist: Yes.

Barney Hill: After ten. Was I there?

Hypnotist: Right here.

Barney Hill: Where's my ciga...was I going to grab cigarettes?

Hypnotist: You look that way Go ahead and get one.

Barney Hill: I thought I was going to come in here and you requested me to take the seat in this one, that chair, and I thought I was reaching to smoke a cigarette but I didn't reach for it.

Hypnotist: How would you describe yourself?

Barney Hill: I feel good.

Hypnotist: Good. Do you know what transpired in this case?

Barney Hill: I know that you've put me in the trance, and I know the intention behind it, but I'm not...

Hypnotist: Okay, we'll go on with this week, one week after today.

***

The next session will be:

Hypnotist What did you observed on the road?

Barney Hill: I saw men in a group who were standing on the highway . They were there and assisted me.

Hypnotist: Who was the person who helped you?

Barney Hill: These men.

Hypnotist: Did they help you to get out of the vehicle? What did you say?

Barney Hill: Yes. I'm just making mental images while my eyes are shut and I believe I am heading down a slight slope but my feet aren't hitting the rocks. It's funny, I was thinking about my feet hitting the rocks. They're moving up with ease, however I'm afraid of opening my eyes as I'm being told repeatedly by my self to shut my eyes. Do not let them open. And...I would not like to be manipulated.

Hypnotist: Don't want to be manipulated. What do you think about when the operation appealing to you?

Barney Hill: I don't know.

Hypnotist: Were you thinking about this driving on the road?

Barney Hill: I was thinking about this while I lay upon my stomach.

Hypnotist: Where were sleeping on the stomach?

Barney Hill: I...I thought I was inside something , however I'm afraid to close my eyes. I was told to shut my eyes.

Hypnotist: Who said that?

Barney Hill: The... man.

Hypnotist: What's the deal?

Barney Hill: That I was able to see through the binoculars.

Hypnotist: Was that one of the guys on the road?

Barney Hill: No.

Hypnotist: Who were these people on the road? What was their role in this?

Barney Hill: They took me and carried me to this ramp.

Hypnotist: Do you feel you would be treated?

Barney Hill: No.

Hypnotist: Do you ever feel that you would be targeted by any means?

Barney Hill: No. I was lying on the table, and I noticed that my fly was hanging open. Then I thought, 'are they making a cup of my privates?' it stopped and I thought, that's hilarious.

Hypnotist: Speak slightly more clearly, please.

Barney Hill: I thought that was hilarious; if I stay still and quiet, I will not be hurt and the whole thing is over. I you are walking and walking...and you're I am being guided, and my eyes are shut and I look up and I see the car, and the lights are not on and it's not moving and Delsey is sitting in the seat. I went under and brushed her. she's in a tight ball beneath the seat. I then sit back and look around. Betty is walking down the road. she enters the car. I'm smiling at her and she's smiling back at me, and we are both happy and satisfied and I'm thinking it's not that bad. It's hilarious I had no reason to be worried and we look up and I see a full moon, and I giggle and think, there it is. Ha, heh. I'm so happy.

The transcript is now complete.

***

The movie "The UFO Incident' came out in 1975, it was based on real recordings from the hypnosis sessions , however certain key information was left out. Of course, they were unable to include all of the sessions as it would be too lengthy and could have made an uninteresting film. One could be struck by the fact how Barney Hill mentions that the "men" he meets are all red-headed Irishmen and the other one is an Nazi. The film does feature James Earl Jones as Barney telling the audience that one is one of them is a Nazi however, he doesn't refer to his statements that he believed the robbers were stealing his money and does not include this line: "They're men; all with black jackets . I'm not carrying any money. ..."

Here's a classic photo from the 1960's early years that illustrates what young bikers looked like back in the early 1960's:

Take note of the 'Nazi' symbols employed, the 'duck-tail haircuts along with the black jackets. While under hypnosis, Barney can clearly be describing males and not aliens.

In the book "Captured" written by Stanton Friedman and Kathleen Marden[3It is noted in an hypnosis session with Barney sessions Barney is anxious when he spots men wearing a duck-tail haircut, and is worried they may be criminals. He is expecting hostile responses but is relieved discover that there isn't any hostility.

The image that Barney did draw under hypnosis goes as like this:

Barney identified the men as the following:

"The figures, as per Barney Hill, were of human shape, wearing shiny black uniforms and capes with peaks or bill marks on their heads (which could be visible when the heads of the figures were turned).

The uniforms resembled glossy leather. (Under the influence of hypnosis the man. Hill said only the "leader" was wearing the shiny black uniform or coat and a sloping cap. The rest of the group had light-colored shirts that were similar to blue jeans, and without caps.)"[4]

Now, compare the description Barney described to the well-known typical images of bikers:

Caps, leather 'uniforms' and goggles. The picture of an alien leader Barney created under hypnosis doesn't appear less alien.

One must also be aware that Barney actually served during World War ll. He'd have plenty of memories from the time too. Black scarfs, black goggles and Nazi emblems were also prevalent among German WWll pilots.

Barney also claimed under hypnosis, they helped him. Barney says, "I saw a group of people and they were sitting on the highway, when they appeared and helped me". Why would he refer to them as a men's group in the event of something alien-like?

In any event it is important to remember that the descriptions of abductions are taken from hypnosis sessions. The first reports they submitted to the military consisted of the witnesses seeing a UFO but didn't mention at all of being taken away. They even mentioned seeing aliens. Betty later claimed that Barney would not like to be viewed as a "crackpot" if Barney told stories of men in UFOs.

The 26th of September in 1961, just one week after her accident, Betty Hill wrote a letter to Major Donald Keyhoe. The writer had read his book , 'The Flying Saucer Conspiracy' and was keen to find more details about flying saucers. Her letter provides an excellent account of her experiences. Here is the transcription of her letter:

Dear Mr. Keyhoe:

The reason for this email is double-sided. We would like to know whether you've written additional books about flying objects prior to when The Flying Saucer Conspiracy was released.

If yes you do, it would appreciate it if you could provide us with details of your publisher, as we've had difficulty getting any information more current than the one in this book. A self-addressed, stamped envelope is provided to make it easier for you.

My husband and I have been very interested in this issue because we had quite an awe-inspiring experience which is different from the other stories that we have heard of. Around midnight on the 20th of September we drove through an National Forest area in the White Mountain, in N.H. It is a deserted area that is largely uninhabited. We first notice an object of light in the sky that appeared to be moving at a rapid pace. We stopped the car and walked out to view the object more closely using our binoculars. It suddenly shifted from north to southwest, and seemed to be moving in a very irregular pattern. We drove on, after stopping to observe it, we saw the following pattern of flight.

The object was spinning and appeared to be illuminated only one side, which caused it to twinkle. When it was close to our vehicle and we stopped, we stopped. While it hung over the top of us it looked like a like a pancake, ringed.with windows in the front that let us see the bright blue-white light. At once, two red lights appeared on either side. My husband was on the road, looking closely. ';--He noticed wings protruding from each side, and the red lights were visible on the tips of the wings.

As it slid closer, the observer could see the inside of the object, but not in a close manner. He could see a number of figures running around as if they were making an hurried preparation. One of them was watching us through the windows. From a distance, when it was apparent that the figures appeared to be the size of a pencil and looked to be wearing some kind of black, shiny uniform.

At this moment, my husband became stunned and retreated to the car in a state of shock in laughter, repeating the threat to take us captive. He drove the car as the motor was in operation. When we began to move we heard a series of beeping or buzzing sounds that were akin to hitting the trunk of our vehicle.

We didn't see the object departing, however we did not notice it again. However, approximately thirty miles to the south , we were once again greeted with the same sound.

The next day , we did submit a account for one Air Force officer, who appeared to be extremely fascinated by the red lights and wings. We did not make a report of my husband's observations of the interior because it appears too amazing to be real.

We are trying to find any clues that could aid my husband to remember what he saw that made him become agitated. The mind of my husband is completely blank at this moment. Any attempt to recall it makes him feel very scared. We are looking into the possibility of hiring a qualified psychiatrist who employs hypnosis.

The flying object was as big. as a motorized four-wheeled plane. The flight was quiet and the light coming inside did not reflect back onto the ground. There doesn't seem to have been anything damaging to our vehicle due to the sound of beeping.

We have both been scared by the experience however, we are also enthralled. We have a strong desire to revisit the location at which this happened in the hopes that we'll meet with the object. We are aware that this chance is not a lot and we must have more information about changes in the past six years.

Any recommendations for reading would be appreciated. Your book was a tremendous help to us as well as an assurance that we're among the few who have had an engaging and educational experience.

Yours truly ,

Mrs. Barney Hill

(Mrs.) Barney Hill

The letter Betty wrote seems to be genuine and authentic with no indications of exaggeration or embellishment. In my research efforts to find the most information I can about this particular case I'd have concluded that the Hills had an experience that is very similar to the account of the incident that Betty Hill gave in the above letter. It seems that the hypnosis sessions resulted in a huge amount of what I'd like to describe as "scrambled" memories.

The other factor that has scrambled, obscured or otherwise made it difficult to tell the story of their story was the reality that as the time went by detail of the experiences continued to grow larger and more amazing. Unfortunately, Barney Hill passed away quite young, at the age of 46 in 1969. Betty lived to the age of 85, and died in 2004. It seems that she added more details throughout the years that could be a result of different memories and subjective interpretations of things. This is evident in the very rare interview she gave in the month of October 1999; the transcript was never published before. I've included this article:

A Rare Interview with Betty Hill in 1999:

Interviewer: We're speaking to Betty Hill, famous and the first abductee. September 19th, in 1961. Betty was driving along together with husband Barney was driving towards the south from Canada...

Betty Hill: Right.

Interviewer: ...when very early in the morning, you noticed an odd light behind the vehicle. It was the 19th of September. What time was Betty at the time that this light behind the car was visible?

Betty Hill: Well, we crossed to New Hampshire and I think we began to see lights, but at the beginning, I noticed an intense glow in the sky. I believed that I had discovered an alien planet until it began to move. This was at around 11 or 10:30 at night. We stopped the car and went out to check what it was, and we believed it was a plane. It was a flight. We stopped our car, took a walk to inspect the plane, which is when it changed directions and began moving towards us. This is in the Lancaster region; then we followed it for approximately 30 miles and then it chased our vehicle.

Interviewer Answer: And as you were discussing it "what's this? What's it?

Betty Hill: Yes, Barney tried to figure out, know planes, but he was trying identify the plane. And it's moving in a very unpredictable manner. It's very odd for us, however this is 1961. It's possible that we could have UFOs, but at the time, we called flying saucers. We were not aware of what a flying spacecraft looked like, but in no way scared or trepidation, we were looking for the craft.

Interviewer: You're through the streets You decide to stop, Barney gets out of the car...

Betty Hill: Actually that was located in the Indian Head area.

Interviewer: Okay, was I in the middle of something when you came across aliens, or was this after.

Betty Hill: This is the next step.

Interviewer: Okay.

Betty Hill: In the Indian Head area, I'm trying to draw the attention of the craft. I'm saying, "C'mon into the room, hi! ,'...I I've got the window closed, I'm shouting"Hi Ho, who are you?' At this point it went off at the top of the hill, climbed across the highway and stopped mid-air before us. probably about fifty feet up in the sky. That's why Barney took out the binoculars to find the craft. When he looked up, at a window that was circular with a bright light in the background it. He then saw men standing in front of the window staring at him from the side. Then the craft started to fall and he became scared. Ran back to his car , saying that he thought the craft was trying to get him.

So we hopped into the car and started speeding along the highway in order to avoid being captured. As we drove along, there's a sound that beeps; like something hit the trunk of the car , and the car shook. Then we drove for another 30 miles before Barney left the road and went to an unrelated road. Then we saw the same group of men that we'd observed on the craft sitting in the middle of the road. They were walking the way we were on and of course we needed to get started in our vehicle. They came as two teams, and took our car out and then walked through the woods and came back to the area where the craft was buried in the ground.

Interviewer: At this moment bizarre thoughts started to run through your head, thoughts that weren't yours. Did you experience any kind of telepathic connection with these entities, or...

Betty Hill: All our communications were verbal.

Interviewer: Verbal?

Betty Hill: Right.

Interviewer: Oh, interesting.

Betty Hill: Yup, they spoke English in a limited manner as a foreigner who is to us and not conversant to our culture.

Interviewer: And at the same time, using typical expressions like"You'll come back soon or something of that or similar.

Betty Hill: Yeah, I guess at the beginning of the section, they put us under some sort of control. I managed to get myself out, but Barney was able only to get himself at least partially; which means that I was about as aware like I am today.

Interviewer: They take through the door of the craft on the ramp. The craft that lands, this is located right off the road 3 ..., but you weren't aware of the exact location at that moment.

Betty Hill: Uh yeah just off Route 3.

Interviewer carry you down this hill, you're taken into the building, and they're able to tell you what they were planning to have to do?

Betty Hill: well, when we arrived at the front door, I decided not going to enter, so I hit him.

Interviewer: Did you punch the entity?

Betty Hill: Yeah, in reality, I engaged in so much effort into it in my gown that it was damaged. He told me, 'come on, all we're looking for is take a quick test and when the tests are completed, you'll be back in your vehicle and be off on your way'.

Interviewer: Let's return to the previous types of creatures, they were the classic alien grey shapes...

Betty Hill: No...

Interviewer Answerer: No, they were not...

Betty Hill: They were humans. They were a species of humans.

Interviewer The interviewer said that they were a type that was human. Did they have cat-like eyes? Chesire-like eyes?

Betty Hill: They had bigger eyes than we do Small nose, tiny lips, and no protruding portion of the ear and they had no hair. They were normal people.

Interviewer: Nothing compares to the classic greys you will...

Betty Hill: I've never had the pleasure of seeing those.

Interviewer The interviewer: OK, there was an executive.

Betty Hill: We gave them different names to distinguish them. It's unclear whether he was the one who led or an interpreter, but we named him the leader. And the person who performed the test, we named"examination. There were nine other people who remained outside in the corridor. We identified them as crew members.

Interviewer: Ok, you're aboard. Do you remember the things you saw as you first entered the craft. You must have been taken off guard, and you thought "this is awesome" or 'what kind of craft do I have'. What can you say about what you can recall from your collective memory?

Betty Hill: Went in to a hallway and I was led into the room. I was required to climb up to the floor was on the same level, and the top of the floor, was higher than the corridor. It was an oval-shaped door that we could find on a ship.

Interviewer: Do remember the moment? Did they set out their plan at that time? Did you go in right away to take the test or...

Betty Hill: They were strict about it the airport; they were actually trying to know if we were alike to them or how we were different from them physically.

Interviewer: Did you believe that you were selected by God or did you are in the wrong place at the wrong moment? Or in the right place at the right moment?

Betty Hill: Well, I'm assuming it was the best time and in the right location However, I believe that we did it myself, and I know that I was waving at them, yelling at them,'Who is this person? All.

Interviewer: When you enter the exam room, but you're isolated from Barney.

Betty Hill: Right. They move him to another room.

Interviewer: Your exam, and all this is brought out in dreams later and hypnosis, but when you take off your clothing and then perform what happens? You'll need to do it be soiled by the fables of abduction tales.

Betty Hill: I don't have any information about those stories.

Interviewer: It's okay and you're much better off.

Betty Hill: But ah I was taken to the first room, and it was empty. There was an unassuming table, an stool, and finally the wall. There were doors in the wall which could move back and forth, and then they placed me onto the stool. Then they, and they checked my ears, eyes and throat and my feet. They also checked my hands and then placed my body on the table and informed me that they would be checking the nervous system of my body. They also used some sort of apparatus to perform this. Then he attempted to insert a needle into my navel, which caused me pain, so they stopped it. Then, uh, the medical examiner left and returned to the room in which Barney was.

Interviewer: Can describe the events that occurred to Barney? What did Barney was able to recall under hypnosis time ago, and what was happening simultaneously in his exam room?

Betty Hill: Uh, with Barney the majority of the examination was similar, except that they were focused on the bone structure of his body and felt all the way up and along his back, arms and everything else, in essence.

Interviewer: Does Barney remember any battle similar to the one you experienced?

Betty Hill: No. They put him under control, he suffered from the most difficult time. It was extremely upset for him as he was unable to move.

Interviewer: So, had put in place paralysis, a temporary paralysis of Barney to control him. In contrast, to you, they gave you an extra bit of freedom as in the sense that you weren't...

Betty Hill: Well I'm tiny. I was smaller than the others, and didn't experience massive amounts of paralysis.

Interviewer: They saw him as more of a threat possibly.

Betty Hill: He was taller than them, bigger.

Interviewer: Okay. After your exam is over, what happens next?

Betty Hill: Well, as the examiner was conducting Barney's test I began to talk with the instructor and said, "I know you're not from the planet, but where do you come coming from?" And he showed me a star map , and he went over a portion of the map to me for a short time after which we discussed food and other aspects of our lives here.

Interviewer: Then what? Do you have any suggestions...

Betty Hill: Actually what brought me to food was when the examiner rushed back to the room in which I was, and began tugging against my teeth. And (chuckle) the examiner wanted to understand why Barney's tooth was removable while mine weren't.

Interviewer: The story is that Barney was wearing dentures?

Betty Hill: Yup, during World War Two, Barney was way too close to hand grenadeand the grenade smashed his teeth.

Interviewer: They were completely confused by all this.

Betty Hill: That was quite puzzling to them.

Interviewer: and humorous. Do you have any other examples of something as a human that you considered to be so universal that you had no idea about it, and that you were confused about; almost childlike that is similar to the denture issue? Is there any other incident similar to it, and they appeared to be a little childish? this? Do you remember?

Betty Hill: Well I was a bit disappointed, I didn't have any knowledge of Their solar system. I'm sure they expected me to to recognize the map.

Interviewer: They were unhappy that you couldn't recognise their house. Let's go to Marjorie Fish months later or several years later, actually under the influence of hypnosis. Try to convince you to be hypnotized to draw the star map.

Betty Hill: Nope, no Betty Hill: No, no, no.

Interviewer The interviewer: Ok, maybe you could go over the matter.

Betty Hill: Dr. Simon in the past, Benjamin Simon, said that during the week If I had the desire, I could recall the star map and I would draw it. But , as I did not think about it, but my hands would be able to go ahead and draw it. Which I did. This was 1965.

Interviewer: Fourteen years after the incident.

Betty Hill: Yeah, it was 1969. Marjorie Fish came here and was here for several days. She she asked me all sorts of questions, for endless hours, which he recorded. And used the tapes to go to the house and do some investigation and identified the locations.

Interviewer: The location in the Star Map, which she claimed was located within the constellation that we call Reticulus which is the name of the system that is Zeta Reticuli and from that point on do you remember the mention of Zeta Reticuli terminology or was this something that we Earthlings have handed them.

Betty Hill: I would not know what they could have called our planet of origin.

Interviewer: Do remember what kind of star system? Was it an white star, a red giant, yellow star or do you remember the type of star you saw or something else?

Betty Hill: I don't know but I know there are astronomers who believe the stars that I've drawn were the most likely to be alive as well as planets that live.

Interviewer: Could they have younger starlets? Hotter stars.

Betty Hill: Actually, we're thought to be between four to six billion years old.

Interviewer: 20 billion. It seems that we get older by a billion every five years...

Betty Hill: But actually Zeta Reticuli is, as we think but we're not certain, but we think it's approximately 11 billion years old. They've been around for a lot longer than we are.

Interviewer: Twice. Over two times as long and the chance to "evolve" and to ...so this puzzling event is that you're questioned, and you're taken on a tour the spaceship, the craft, or something else that's not on a 'need to know' basis?

Betty Hill: No, only one room was the one I was in.

Interviewer: The conversation with you and your question and answer session was much more than Barney and they didn't provide Barney an opportunity to ask questions.

Betty Hill: No, absolutely not, there was no discussion with Barney. I was having fun and had a great time. He laughed, we joked.

Interviewer: Really.

Betty Hill: Yup, I asked him to come back. I asked, "please, please, return, please, there are so many people that would be delighted to get to know you."

Interviewer: It wasn't any kind of traumatizing experience.

Betty Hill: No.

Interviewer said: It was a revealing experience. Perhaps spiritually inspiring.

Betty Hill: Right; no one can say there's no living life elsewhere on the planets. (laughs)

Interviewer The interviewer: At that same moment, it is believed that it was 36 hours since the sighting; it's recorded according to Jacques Valleee at 2:44 AM. Pease Air Force had been pursuing an unidentified object.

Betty Hill: Oh yeah I told him that. Pease Air Force Base released the report on radar where they observed this craft. They two planes were sent out to look it over and the reports of pilots are classified, so we know who the chumps are.

Interviewer: To the skeptical this kind of blows them off their feet in the event that you make up a story out of thin air You really know what you're talking about or it's very well-planned event to contain Pease personnel involved. And to claim the story of Betty and Barney are the same person. Barney was employed as a postal worker?

Betty Hill: Yeaup.

Interviewer is a postal worker, your company is involved with real estate, and has pulled off a major fraud using the air force. It's near impossible, if it's not even impossible. I think absurd is the word I'm looking for. After you've been released from the craft after which you return to the car, you go through your watches, what's the reason?

Betty Hill: Well, I don't believe we checked our watches until nearing home, and we wanted to know the time and both of our watches were malfunctioning.

Interviewer: How can you not explain the amount of time that has that has passed?

Betty Hill: We realized that the journey had taken longer than what it was supposed to take perhaps two hours.

Interviewer: Did you feel dizzy, do you have headaches, did you feel physically ill, did you feel tired What were your feelings? Can you explain what your experience was?

Betty Hill: We'd been traveling all night, and we returned home at about 5 in the morning. We were relaxed, calm, and being very well.

Interviewer: Didn't you experience any trauma or injury at any point?

Betty Hill: No.

Interviewer: Should I say that I was violated at the moment?

Betty Hill: (shakes her head but does not shake it))

Interviewer: You get in your home, and in the morning, you go to check the car. What do you see when you examine the vehicle?

Betty Hill: Clearly polished spots on the trunk of the car. That day, it was getting a tropical downpour due to a hurricane moving through. It was the downpour was heavy and did not affect the spots in any way. The spot remained for several months.

Interviewer: What was your sister's story whom you claimed witnessed an UFO advised you to take a step? in the vehicle?

Betty Hill: Oh, it was a physicist that advised us to take a compass out and look around for those places that we visited.

Interviewer: What did you hear?

Betty Hill: and the compass was extremely, very unstable.

Interviewer: Was she spinning?

Betty Hill: Yeah, (makes circular hand movement back and forth) We tried it on various parts of the vehicle and it didn't work.

Interviewer: I think it was close to the area where the spots were?

Betty Hill: Yes.That's right.

Interviewer: If the inference is an anomaly in magnetics, which was causing distortion to the magnetic pull that the compass. After that you call the CUFO's J Allen...

Betty Hill: No.

Interviewer What is the order of things?

Betty Hill: First of all, we didn't take any action. In the next step, when I was at NICAP in Washington I wrote them, because I was curious about being exposed to UFOs at close-range, did you experience any health issues? If exposed by radiation? What type of health risks?

Interviewer: They sent Walter Webb as their representative. This letter ends up with NICAP as well as The Centre for UFO studies, Dr. J. Allen Hynek.

Betty Hill: It might havehappened, but I don't know.

Interviewer: Have you never, ever, ever spoke to the Dr. Hynek?

Betty Hill: Oh no We did. We were great friends but that was many some time further on. We appeared on numerous TV shows together.

Interviewer Question: What was your impression regarding the Dr. Hynek, was he clearly a thinly disguised Skeptic?

Betty Hill: Oh no Oh no! No, no. He believed in every phrase of it.

Interviewer The interviewer: At the close.

Betty Hill: As soon when he was met by.

Interviewer: It appears that his view on the UFO phenomenon came after was humiliated by the "swamp gas" issue and then drew an absurd argument before the college dorm, I'm assuming in Michigan The Great Lakes, that's when He said enough was enough. The government was masked or at the very least spouting false information and disinformation about UFO phenomenon.

Betty Hill: Of course when he said that it was because he worked in the federal government.

Interviewer The interviewer: So you know that Dr. Hynek and you were wonderful friends back then.

Betty Hill: Oh yeah. Yup and his son was born the road in Massachusetts.

Interviewer: So, you're having trouble in your dreams right now. What happens at home.

Betty Hill: Actually, 10 nights following this incident I had a string of dreams. For five nights each one was unique, and later realized was a memory of the events that had occurred.

Interviewer: In your dreams, you were describing the dream you were describing to me?

Betty Hill: (Nodding yes) Yes.

Interviewer: At this point, what should you do? Are you sure that Barney having issues with this? Does Barney is his life pattern changed?

Betty Hill: No.

Interviewer Asks: Has his mood changed in any way.

Betty Hill: Actually, the first thing I did was in the next day I wrote down all the details I remembered of my fantasies.

Interviewer: The next day, that would be the 20th.

Betty Hill: And every time, but it wasn't the same night after.

Interviewer: We're talking about roughly between the 20th and the 30th of the month.

Betty Hill: Yeah, and I wrote, I recorded an album.

Interviewer: Thirty-eight Years ago.

Betty Hill: And then I took them off and the items and put them away. Later, about months later, I spoke with my supervisor about what I was thinking about in terms of the meaning of dreams. She then replied, "Well, maybe it was a dream that happened."

Interviewer and the interviewer suggested...

Betty Hill: We just had a conversation about it.

***

You can clearly see that Betty's perception of events that occurred 38 years earlier has drastically changed from her initial impressions she relayed to Donald Keyhoe one week after the incident. (The rest of her interview from 1999 is available inside the Appendix.)

The drastic shift in a first-hand account is can be expected The memories we are able to recall of our childhood traumatic events tends to change with time and people are often surprised to discover the difference in their memories of an event in comparison to the memories of their grandparents or parents. Add the passing of time, deep illusions and the interpretation of dreams that is subjective and you've got yourself the recipe for more confusion and erratic behavior. How often do people think of events which turn out to be real-life events that were subconsciously forgotten? I'm pretty sure the majority of my fantasies are the result of a mix of fantasy fragments of actual experiences and indirect reflections of personal experiences. But this is just me.

Despite the changes in Betty's narrative over time, and despite the massive amount of coverage given to this case, both positive as well as negative, it's still one of the most important and groundbreaking incidents in the timeline of Alien Abduction research.

Another possible Theory

Naturally, I haven't attempted to analyze all the other details of the story, including Betty's star map and The Blue Book reports, the many documented interviews, and more. I'll let readers to look into these aspects that have been thoroughly described in the reference materials that are listed in the Bibliography.

Before I finish this chapter on Betty as well as Barney Hill, I would like to propose a different theory that was never previously explored.

Research has shown that the Hill's started their journey by taking an excursion through Niagara Falls and Montreal and returning home. It appears that their spontaneous getaway ended up going off the rails when it was still in Montreal. They were able to remember window shopping on St. Catherine Street but shortly thereafter, they became lost, requested directions several times (once from an officer) and chose to drive home on their own, non-stop, since they were afraid they would not find an apartment that would take their pet. They have munchies twice when they get home, but they continue driving through the night.

The route from Montreal through Indian Head, New Hamshire

It is interesting to know that at that period (1961) research was carried out in the Allan Memorial Institute in Montreal located situated just two blocks to the west from St. Catherine Street, close to any parking spot they could have been parked. These tests, which included those using LSD was conducted under the now notorious MKUltra Program that was run by the CIA. Do I need to continue or do you think it's possible to find the connections?

The program wasn't limited to LSD The researchers also tested different drugs that had some of the effects listed below:

1 - Substances that cause impulsiveness and indecision until the individual receiving the substance is discredited in the public.

2. Substances that may change a person's perception of reality.

3. Substances that enhance the effects of alcohol on one's body. (The Hills admitted to partially drinking a six-pack of booze while on their travels.)

4. Substances that result in memory loss or amnesia. Etcetera...

You'll get the picture. The Hills didn't provide a clear justification for their excursion in the first place. The trip is described as a honeymoon trip, but they were married for 16 months before but you wouldn't describe that as a post honeymoon getaway would you?

Barney has stated that it was a spur-of an opportunity surprise to Betty however, why the chaos and confusion that erupted in the city of Montreal even though he carried maps on his person? It could be that the Hill's were the victims of a devious experiment without their consent or knowledge? They were apparently strapped for cash traveling with just $70 cash. Perhaps Barney discovered a way earn some cash quickly in the Allan Memorial Institue by participating in a few innocent tests. Since he was a former military officer, he may be a perfect candidate. If you're planning the time to enjoy a leisurely drive, you wouldn't take a drive to Lincoln, New Hampshire to Montreal, Quebec and back. It is likely that they were traveling to Montreal because of a specific motive.

I was a part of a few times within Montreal my own time in the 80's . I often heard about student applicants for medical tests for cash-flow boosts at various places. (The MKUltra program was mothballed in the late 80's.)

I know this alternative theory is a bit of a stretch, but people who act rationally typically don't drive for 16 hours straight in an inaccessible area to have enjoyment. Remember Barney's last comment under the hypnosis effect "I can see that Betty is on the road and she jumps in the car and I'm smiling at her, and she's looking at me with a smile and we are both joyful and satisfied and I'm thinking this isn't all that bad. What a great story I didn't have any reason to worry and then we glance and I see a brilliant moon, and I laugh and think, there it is. Heh, ha, and I'm so happy". Do you think that it sounds like they were just a bit satisfied? Certain of their stories during hypnosis bear all the characteristics of an acid trip that is bad that is, paranoia, confusion and a misperception of reality. It could have been LSD or a specific mix of drugs being test-driven.

Additionally, I'm just mentioning this theory in an attempt to maintain the mind open. In the end, the Hill's aren't here to defend themselves. My intention is not to smear any person or to suggest they took drugs in a shady way It's my intention to keep my thoughts open because the truth can be different from fiction. Would you travel for all day long for entertainment? Perhaps no, but if you were aware that you could earn hundreds of dollars for just a quick visit to a medical clinic, this could alter your motive when you're done. And once you've finished, you'd like to return home as soon as you could.

The entire story of the MKUltra program is amazing at first, and yet, it is documented that it happened. It is clear that the Hill's experienced the most unique and terrifying event, yet the details of what happened to them aren't clear and subject to speculation. It is up for the reader to make the conclusions they want to draw.

Chapter 2: Tell Tale Signals Of Abduction

Based on the Dr. Brad Steiger, a well-known author of a variety of books on alien abduction, which include The UFO Abductors and a researcher on research on alien abduction If you've had the experience of being taken to a certain place but you are unable to connect the dots of the reason and how you were there, it's an indication that you've been taken by aliens.

Being held in a prison cell by paranormal creatures usually leaves an eerie memory. Sharing the story with a acquaintance about the alleged alien abduction, particularly someone who doesn't believe in being able to believe in aliens is not a great decision. It is possible to be dismissed as being deluded and be sarcastic and suggest that you be admitted to a mental hospital.

To avoid being viewed as an embarrassing subject To avoid being ridiculed, be able to keep your worries about alien abduction to you. Instead of making assumptions, figuring out the signs of the bizarre encounter is the best option.

The Abductee's Marks

Sometimes, alongside the strong and empty feeling that you've been taken by aliens, are new wounds and cuts on your arm, ankle wrist, or other body parts. Because they're small, the most common response is to ignore the wounds as minor. Why should you be concerned over a small scratch when it could disappear in a few days? But, if you give some thought to it, even the smallest of blemishes due to their appearance unsettling, could be worrying.

Aliens and Alien Abduction Hints

If the belief that you've been abducted by aliens continues, you can look up the list of alien abduction clues which have been put together by abduction and alien life researchers. Find out if other people have been through the same experiences similar to yours. Maybe, by knowing that there are similar claims to yours, you'll be confident that you're not the only ones on this path.

20 clues of an alien abduction

1. A sudden interest in UFOs and aliens.

2. After being reported missing

3. After being spotted wearing a hood, that you're not aware of

4. Experiences of mysterious absences within an hour or less

5. Have inexplicably bloody spots on your sheets

6. Aversion to the subject of UFOs

7. Feeling intensely that you are continuously watched

8. Feeling intensely that your body has been through solid objects

9. Reacting with intense intensity to images of aliens

10. Remembering the flight memories

11. Nose-bleeds without any particular reason

12. Dreaming of aliens in recurring sequences

13. After having sat across an unidentified person sitting at the table

14. After having seen a UFO, I've had the pleasure of seeing one.

15. Self-esteem issues

16. Have you seen flashes of light at your house

17. After having seen strange smoke lights

18. You've woken up in a room that you don't recall having been asleep in

19. I woke up in a panicked state without a reason

20. You've woken up with an inexplicable sensations in your Genitals

Chapter 3: Common Abduction Account

Alien abduction researchers like John E Mack and Thomas E. Bullard have said that despite the fact that each abduction report is unique in terms of specifics, a similar way of communicating a message can be found in the accounts. After further investigation they can reveal a story that is similar to those previously described.

A portion of the most common claims of alien abduction are considered quite absurd to the common people; they aren't considered to be credible. Only researchers studying alien life and those who believe that extra-terrestrial beings, are the ones to view the claims in a mocking manner. From the perspective of the most fervent group given that instances of paranormal activity are documented and reported, progress on research on alien abductions and other related research projects could be anticipated. Therefore, they keep encouraging people who had previously experienced strange encounters to share their stories and share their experiences.

Captivity

A person abducted who gives an abduction narrative typically begins by describing the manner in which he was taken. In the beginning it is normal to recount the moment when the abductee was unable to resisting. While he may fight to resist the abductor's plan but he physically is unable to do so, as is usually observed.

Time Loss

Time loss is an atypical component of an abduction claim by aliens. An absence that is inexplicably long, lasting between 2 and 3 hours is typically described. Because of various reasons (e.g. anxiety, medical intervention as well as shock at being in a new setting) This portion of the account can be bleak and is usually a mess, excluding the amount of hours listed.

According to those who were abducted, whether or not they remember the exact events they experienced while in captivity, they feel strongly that they appeared to have been secluded for a few hours. If a friend can verify that, their claims they will become more controversial.

Tests

Most of the time alien abductees are willing to go through intense psychological and physical tests. This allows them to back up their claims and avoid doubts about the credibility of their claims.

In the event that they do not want to undergo tests and do not take part in this section of the typical abduction report it is possible that they are viewed as to be unreliable. Particularly, if they've been summoned from authorities. Their refusal to defy certain procedures may indicate that their assertions are not true.

Conference

The abduction report typically examines the exchange that occurred. Information about the method for communication as well as the place of the meeting and the type of messages exchanged are documented. The likelihood is that an abductee may claim that no specific language (i.e. dialects which both the parties comprehend) was spoken, however regardless of the absence of acceptable communication measures, an agreement was nevertheless reached.

Guide

If the memory of an abductee is well, he'll be able to recount the beginning of what happened when he was with the abductor. Was he commanded to get on the spaceship? Was the location he'd been held in bright? Was the only prisoner in the area or did he observe other prisoners similar to him? Did he get taken prisoner by non-human creatures who wore colored spacesuits?

But, since the vast majority of reports of abductions by aliens have abductees who are unable to recall even the tiniest bit of what happened at the time the kidnapping occurred, an average report of abduction by aliens leaves out any specific details about the source of the information.

Return

A detailed account of an alien abduction will include information about the return of an abductee. The abduction may have made the person feel like the person was transported to a location that was miles away or even to an area within his immediate neighborhood and he'll have it documented. As far as he is able to abilities the subject will be able to describe the manner in which he was returned to the place he was originally.

The Repercussions

Because an abduction by aliens can be extremely stressful and traumatic, a typical abduction report is not complete without the consequences. In this portion of the report the psychological and physical changes the abductee was forced to endure are detailed.

The effects of an alien abduction is determined by how the victim is able to cope. The ability of the person being abducted to adjust and adapt to a new outlook on life is evident.

Chapter 4: Abduction & Science

However much evidence that is provided by the aliens and UFO researchers, the majority of people across the globe are skeptical about being skeptical of the possibility that aliens are real as well as even the likelihood of abductions by aliens. This proves that for many that even science cannot change their opinion regarding the subject.

Although, as scientists claim, enough scientific explanations have been offered, the majority of people still question whether or not the stories of abductions by aliens are true. From their viewpoint they believe that the claims of encounters with extraterrestrials are just a way to create excitement.

But, with the help of evidence of their beliefs, believers in the paranormal are able to remain true to their claims. If they choose to pursue more research into the subject and have evidence been provided by friends can be a strong argument. With the scientific evidence they have gathered they will know the best place to start and where to go.

Stockholm Syndrome What is It?

Researchers from ICAR and others studying abductions by aliens, have shown that almost all people who are abducted by aliens have Stockholm Syndrome. They also note that their bizarre experience of encountering extraterrestrials is what has caused them to experience strange feelings towards their abductor.

Due to the alleged alien interaction with another person, they have a strong need to express their sympathy and empathy to their fellows. Particularly, if it's out of the norm for a person to be expressive and communicative this is a bit questionable. According to the research, it suggests that there's an evolution in behaviour.

The existence of Alien Life

According to research conducted by alien life scientists as well as experts from the most reputable astrobiology associations abductions by aliens are real. The majority of people who have claimed to have been held by aliens aren't just making up stories. Because these claims can be confirmed by scientific evidence after more investigation, their stories can be interpreted as evidence of a paranormal existence.

Two clues to how alien life could exist

1. Canals on Mars

The canals that are found on Mars suggest that there are occupants on the planet. It suggests that waterways were constructed.

In actual fact, Percival Lowell, an American astronomer who constructed the Arizona Lowell Observatory in 1894 and sketched the canals that lie on Mars through observing the surface of Mars with his telescope. According to him on careful examination of his drawings, you will notice that straight lines are constructed.

2. Cyanobacteria on meteorite

Cyanobacteria also known as cyanophyta are bacteria that generate energy through photosynthesis. They are single-celled and blue-green in their color.

Since traces of cyanobacteria have been discovered on a meteorite scientists and astrobiology colleagues such as Professor. Richard Hoover of NASA believe that, since they have biological roots that life exists outside of Earth.

Chapter 5: A Mental Health Assessment Of

The Abductees

According to more than the course of a dozen alien existence or UFO study projects including one conducted by the Dr. Richard Mc Nally, an deterioration in the mental health of the people who have been abducted is evident. In addition to the ridicule that they encounter when telling stories people who believe they've been abducted by aliens are constantly dealing with unacknowledged psychological issues.

Because the experiences of abductions by aliens are not well-known and somewhat painful, you are able to discern where the abductees originate from. If what they experienced is similar to what has happened to you, you could be affected mentally, too.

Paranoid Delusionary Schizophrenia

The victims of alien abductions are believed to suffer from schizophrenia that is paranoid which is a mental disorder that causes one to believe that they are targeted for being in danger or for a reason. This is a serious condition that must be addressed as soon as that is possible. In the absence of treatment, it could cause you to miss important aspects of the world.

After being abducted The abductees are made to believe that they will be taken back to their normal lives in order to carry out a crucial task (i.e. helping the government, or to conduct additional research on alien life). They believe they were destined to return to help the government, since they could be more beneficial within their own universes.

Psychosexual Identity Misrepresentation

The issue of misidentification between sexual partners is a frequent problem that alien abductees have to be worried about. The fact that they were taken from their home in a location they have no idea about and can impact how they desire to be satisfied. Because their captivity has made them separated from their normal life, they are left confused about what they used know about.

No matter if they've been sexually victimized from aliens or abductees often find themselves struggling to make decisions about the sexual preference they have. In certain cases because of the confusion they experience, abductees seek to have sexual encounters with both genders.

Chapter 6: Kidnapped, And Then Narrated

Abductees of aliens as well as alien abduction claimants and even those who experienced them may be criticized after sharing their strange experiences. But, as they say even though they would like to alter their stories to make them more credible (i.e. include elements of the environment) However, placing it in other contexts appears to add to the mythology.

As they freely acknowledge instead of telling a great story, they plan to focus on exposing the truth about abductions by aliens. While all stories differ regarding the manner in which they were abducted and what occurred in their detention however, the stories of all of the abductees provide similar incident that was a paranormal one. They've shared that even though they don't remember the majority of details about their strange experience, they are so strongly about an incident.

It's the Barney Hill and Betty Hill Case

As they drove across Canada from Canada to New Hampshire one night, Barney Hill and his wife, Betty, saw an unknown flying object. While they observed that in comparison to other heavenly objects that it was far from the ordinary, they both thought it was as a star. Up until it made a sharp turn and they didn't think about it as anything other than.

The couple also shared that their experience caused various doubts. They shared a detailed account of their abductors, but shockingly they were unable to describe in a clear way the events that transpired. They recalled that, after the unknown object flew towards them, they repressed memories, and their watches appeared to have stopped working.

The incident, said to have occurred on September 19th, 1961, began to stir the minds of those who lived in the Hills town. When the two men spoke about their bizarre encounter, the public began to become interested in the strange creatures.

Dr. Hopkins Abduction Dr. Hopkins Abduction

Researchers on UFOs and alien life Professor Dr. Budd Hopkins, accounted for brief encounters with strange creatures twice. Because his research to the field are dense, he was ordered to destroy of his notes from the two occasions.

The first time the doctor met was with a person who called him over the phone to set up a meeting. When he confirmed his attendance at the meeting, the person came to his front step. He was then ordered to stop doing his investigation and destroy all evidence.

The second incident according to the doctor's report it, was between a man and a woman who spoke with monotonous voices and didn't appear to have eyebrows, hair and lips. The doctor observed that both continued to make sexually inappropriate remarks.

The Russian Politiker

In the 90s, Kirsan Ilyumzhinov, a multi-millionaire Russian politician, was said that he was held by unknown beings wearing yellow space suits. He was ordered to go into an unlit spaceship in which the spaceship was able to show him before a group of people that he was unable to recognize.

In the course of abduction, he shared thoughts about his passion for the game of chess, and how it can be used to help explain the intricate nature of everyday life. While the phrases which were shared between him and a few others aren't clear and undefined, he did say the fact that there was a consensus in the works.

Chapter 7: The Financial Considerations

Another of the most well-known alien abduction events that has ever been recorded took place in Arizona on the 5th of November in 1975. Travis Walton, Mike Rogers and five other lumberjacks were on their way home from the forest when they saw something they believed was a UFO soaring through the trees. A documentary about the incident produced these details:

Travis Walton:

"Well as I stopped the truck in that spot... There were men were shouting for me to slow down the vehicle. They had seen something off to the left there, evidently following the time we broken through a bunch of pine trees. We looked to our left and there , soaring over the ground for around twenty feet over the ground, and around 100 feet from the truck was a huge shining object."

Travis had jumped from the truck, and had walked forward, and then started walking through it.

Travis Walton:

"I thought that this thing would just fly off and disappear before I could get close. I was quite scared and decided to go after it. When I raised the 'Wham!' flag, something came over me, similar to an actual blow. It felt like an intense, shock-type of sensation. I then fell unconscious."

Mike Rogers: "I jerked my head to find out what the source of this light was, and here's Travis returning to the air. He was able to land a bit further than the spot he was standing. He fell on his back flat. The men in the back were shouting at me for out of the way and I took the gas and was off down the road."

According to Travis his account, the next thing he recalls was getting up in what he described as a vast dark room with a dark floor, and a person lying on a cold platform, and surrounded by alien creatures.

Travis Walton:

"I certainly wasn't in an institution."

Interviewer: Can you explain what the aliens appeared like?

"Well they were humanoid. Like having two legs, two arms similar to that, however, they had extremely large heads, with no hair, like a white, pale grayish skin."

He claims that he was able to recall the large surgical instrument placed on his head and then used to eliminate eye fluid. After his disappearance, within a few days the story of Travis Walton made the news across America. After a long search in the forest, nobody was able to find any evidence about what transpired.

The police suspect that the group may have killed Travis and then destroyed the body. However, Mike and the other members were able to pass polygraph tests and remained to their UFO story.

Interviewer The interviewer: You and the other guys in the vehicle were convinced that you'd witnessed an UFO, and it was taking Travis.

Mike Rogers: "We weren't certain that we'd seen UFOs, but we were certain we'd seen UFO. It was more than just a UFO. It was it was an Unidentified Flying Object; this was a flying object that was definitely visible. It was close, extremely vivid and burned in my mind for the rest of my life."

And then, like he'd left, Travis woke up on the edge of town, just a few minutes away from the location where the UFO had been. He was confused and confused.

Interviewer Asks: How long were you really away for?

"I was absent for five days, six hours and odd minutes. Even when I returned I was under belief that it was only an hour or so I believed I was missing the entire night."

Travis as well as the remaining six suspects went through the most rigorous examinations and tests conducted by experts. Although their tale was as bizarre as it was, nobody could prove that it was a fake or fraudulent.

Travis Walton: "What we observed was not too distant. It was clear that we could see the thing. It was clearly visible, and it was clear. It wasn't just a spot of light in the sky , or anything similar to this. It was extremely close. It was possible to throw an object and hit it. I was scared , but just like everyone else, I took my shoes out and walked toward the rock. It could have been a mistake however I was thinking this possibility could be a thing that would be able to fly away. I was just looking to take more detail and thought that it would disappear. "

Mike Rogers: "After we placed maybe a quarter-mile distance between us occurred to me that I was aware of what we'd done. I thought that my friend had been still there and I'd put him down. That's why I put the truck down. A few of us didn't like that at all. I said , well, we must get back. He might be injured. It is evident that he has been injured. And we can help him. We returned to the location, and the object was gone. Travis was absent. We thought that maybe the guy went somewhere else. Therefore, we conducted a hand-in hand search. You could say that there were six mature men walking in the woods about the same distance as they could. We concluded that we've not been able to locate the guy. If we had to take action to help, what would we do? The only thing we could think of was to call authorities."

The Sheriff was there and was able to listen to their tale. He was cautious, but not entirely incredulous. He decided that the best solution was return up the hill early in the morning and search for Travis.

Mike Rogers: "Three of the men had no plans of returning up the mountain. They wanted to remain right there, where they were. Then me and another fellow and a number of the Sheriff individuals climbed to the top of the hill. We explored all roads that were below and above, we searched for tracks. we searched for signs. We listened but couldn't locate him in any way. No trace was left of him and no footprints whatsoever. It was clear that this object was taking him. who they were, we did not know at the time. Someone else, somewhere in the universe took him, and he was not there."

Mike Rogers and the Sheriff came to inform Walton's mother that their son was missing.

Mike Rogers: "All through the night and over the next few days it was difficult to comprehend. We could not be able to comprehend what had happened. It was hard to comprehend. There was something that had happened, or an odd thing had happened. We didn't know whether it was a disaster or great. We were not sure that it was something we did not comprehend, and that was what taken place and the result was that it was extremely traumatic extremely traumatic, and the most traumatizing event I've ever experienced."

The Sheriff of Holbrook believed that the suspects had killed Travis and then buried their bodies in the woodlands. They were also using the UFO incident as an excuse.

The next day the polygraph examiner issued the official account. They informed Mike Rogers that this was the first time the polygraph examiner was able to handle so many people who were interested in the same incident. The examiner said his findings proved that the men were indeed seeing something that which they believed was UFOs.

Travis Walton: "When I was struck by the numbing pain I went to sleep then within a second I realized was that I had was able to regain consciousness. But not immediately, more slowly. My head wasn't clear. I was in great discomfort. I lay upon my stomach. I was not sure what I was doing. It was... It was then that I recalled the incident that took place within the forest. While I was recovering consciousness, I tried to determine what the cause did and why it was happening. It could be that there was a medical facility, or some other thing as I had been injured.

I was in front of the things that were heading toward me. They stopped, and then stood watching me. They seemed tolook straight at me. I didn't feel any emotion at all The gaze was detached and a kind of observing. It was as if they could see everything I was thinking and even dreaming. It was a very uncomfortable feeling to be that you are so exposed. The huge eyes stared at me, and when they would blink and look at an eyelid that was big, it would slide down and up like windows, opening and closing and my experience. I felt the weirdest kind of sensation. I couldn't bear it. could not bear their eyes."

"There there was an lever in that area. When I moved it the pattern of stars began to shift. This kind of confused me for a moment because, it seemed like I was moving for a moment since something that was shifting in that way. Then I realized I should not be playing with it and, you know, at that point I realized that I was part of some kind of craft and was aware of what had occurred before I realized that I could crash into the thing or do something else. The man was different from the humanoid animals I'd previously seen. This was someone who was human, as an individual wearing blue uniform. I approached him and thought that you knew I was being saved and that I was being saved. It was the thought that this person was someone that you recognize. I began asking all sorts of questions. For example: "Where am I? You were out. Who are these guys I observed? Please talk to me! He led me through a few doors that lead down the hall to an additional room."

Five days passed before Travis returned. He was required to pass an exam to determine if he was lying. He too passed. He had no idea that the event will have a lasting impact on the remainder years of his existence.

Travis: "The thing that has caused more anger and hurt in my life because of this has been the realization that I'm not able to look at me any more. My self as an individual. I feel a sense of invisibilitydue to this phenomenon. Every interaction I make with other people is filtered by the lens of distortion which happened to me, fifty years ago. It's a thing which has happened to me recently. I did not do anything extraordinary or heroic. I'm not a hero or famous person any more than I'm a sly person and... maybe an unorthodox kind of space cadet. I'd rather be recognized as me instead of being viewed in terms of the thing that occurred to me. It could have happened to anyone."

Stanton Friedman (UFO Researcher): "Well, I spent the time with Travis along with Mike Rogers. He did well in the test of lying. Their account is unchanging. Five other people were present who watched all of the incidents unfold. They also completed an examination to detect lies. His claim is invariably true. It hasn't changed. I've found his account to be extremely convincing."

What happened to Travis Walton that night in 1975? What did he and other loggers observe within the woods? Where did Travis disappear over the next five days?

Interviewer: What would you say to those who think"You know, the seven guys have created this entire story?

"Ha! I'm talking about... You know seven people are saying the exact same thing, and they remain true to their claims for more than two decades. We all of us have passed polygraph tests. More than one test in the polygraph category. Each theory that the critics make is a joke It's easy to verified."

Another interesting detail which was not mentioned in the moment. The test for radiation was conducted on the clothing and hats that the group wore during the night. The Geiger counter produced an unusually high reading of a six out of the scale of ten. If this was fake or the result of some kind of mass delusion where did this excessive amount of radiation originate?

Stanton Friedman: "I'm absolutely certain the fact that Travis Walton was indeed abducted. Their accounts are identical. I've listened to the arguments of the loud negativists regarding this storyand, it's almost always the case, they do not appear to be able to stand. After you have a look and do not accept them as gospel.

I'm certain he's telling truth, along with Mike due to the peripheral information and polygraphs."

***

To read the account of this documented incident and watch the reportage depicted in the various'made-for-TV documentaries, it's easy to gain a clear feeling that the incident was well-documented and has actually took place as reported; however, on closer inspection this Travis Walton incident is as much as opaque like mud from water.

The incident has resulted in many pages of evidence. It took me a long time to review all the information from a variety of sources. This is a real issue when it comes to investigating instances in the field of Alien

Abduction; the amount of data and analysis continues to grow as time passes.

A significant portion of the evidence comes from those from Philip J. Klass, who appeared to be working tirelessly in exposing the credibility and character of Mike Rogers. Philip Klass passed away in 2005, and despite having some doubts regarding the topic of UFOs and spacecrafts, he did use attack on character (ad to argue) when speaking with other people. The harshness of his analysis did not make him a popular figure.

After reviewing every piece of evidence I could locate and trying to process it all, I noticed some things that left an impression. Much of the arguments seem to disappear, however, these three issues stand out.

The story first comes in The National Enquirer that includes a image that shows Travis Walton holding up a check for $2,500. Did there exist a financial incentive to these guys to create an account? Klass found all kinds of scathing details about the way Mike Rogers was having difficulty with his obligations to government for work on lumber and how he might have been pressured by the government to not disclose all of his business transactions. The legal cases that involved fraud also came to light , but we should give these guys the benefit of the doubt. The act of slandering someone's character is not very helpful when looking for information. It could be a source of suspicion, but let's say that they were decent, honest, and decent people. It was reported that the National Enquirer would run a contest each year, and award between $5000 and $10,000 for the top UFO story of the year. The contest ended up offering the possibility of a $100,000 prize if evidence was submitted that proved the existence of aliens. What better method to prove that aliens visited than being taken hostage by one?

The suspects met with the Enquirer shortly after the incident. The story was published on the 16th of December issue of 1975 and the account of the men receiving the reward of $5,000 was revealed in the July 13thissue of 1976.

It's impossible to determine whether the men knew about the prize prior to the time the incident happened. In the National Enquirer had a very huge circulation. It is not clear if it was 'common to the majority of people to know about the possibility of a "big payout' in an amazing UFO story, I can only guessthat probably it would be the norm.

The other test is the polygraph which was administered by John McCarthy. The test was mandated from the National Enquirer to be eligible to win the prize cash prize. If the money was a reward to be a winner, it is likely that Travis Walton would have wanted to pass this test as quickly as was possible. (strangely that it was not the first test that was tested - check out the an appendix to find out more about the test that was first completed) This test was administered within ten days of the incident, and 5 days following the time Travis Walton was found, which means that after being gone for five consecutive days. took another five days before he was able to take the test. It was evident that there was very little time lost from the moment that he was discovered until the point of discussion the report with the police about whether he was ineligible to win the money prize. Here's a transcription of the report of the polygraph:

16 November 1975

Re: WALTON, TRAVIS C.

On the 15th of November, Travis C. WALTON was administered a polygraph test in The National Enquirer, at the request of Mr. Paul JENKINS, who was a reference to WALTON's recent UFO encounter. The test began at 1425, and. completed in 1615 hours.

In the course of the test He displayed deceitful behavior on the charts, as he was able to answer the questions that were relevant to him as follows: indicated:

Are you on an aircraft in the vicinity of Hober on the 5th of November? ... "Yes"

Was it true that you were on a spacecraft during 5th-10th of November? ... "Yes".

Have you told Dr. Harder about being in an spacecraft?

... "No".

Did you collaborate with other people to commit an UFO

hoax? ... "No".

Did you cover up any of the GILLESPIE, the sheriff's question regarding

your disappearance? ... "No"

Did you hide somewhere in Arizona when you disappeared?

No"

Have you been urged by anyone else to lie on this test?

"... "No"

His reactions to the test were similar to those of a normal. He appeared to be in a state of lucidity and, prior to taking the test, said that he had a clear understanding of all of the questions that were askedand could respond to each one by an "Yes" as well as "No".

It was evident during the exam that he was consciously trying to alter the pattern of his breathing.

Based on his responses to all charts, it's his opinion by this observer that WALTON along with other people, is trying to make a fake UFO and is not aboard any spacecraft.

John J. MCCARTHY

Examiner

The fact that The Enquirer approached Travis Walton initially or not isn't significant, however their fact they met within a couple of days of the incident issignificant. The evidence of this meeting dispels any statements from those involved who might have suggested that they didn't want to receive any publicity. It is believed that the Polygraph Examiner was under agreement to keep the results confidential but later revealed the results since it was his belief that the results of the test had been published[6] and wanted to avoid the possibility of a fraud. Following this, McCarthy was attacked in different media reports, the results were debated, additional tests for polygraphs (as as the previous) were administered by other examiners and were passed the list goes on. However the test itself remains as a significant source of contention in the whole story.

There is also the issue of interviews that were held in the lead up to Travis Walton being found. When a search was carried out for Travis Walton in the evening of November 8, 1975, a person named Fred Sylvanus, (he was director of the Arizona Regional UFO Project and an active part of Ground Saucer Watch) conducted an interview with Mike Rogers and Duane Walton (Travis his step-brother). This is a brief version of the interview conducted of Fred as well as Duane:

Duane: "I don't believe Duane is injured or hurt or injured in any manner.

He'll be back at some point or other, when they finish the work they're doing."

Sylvanus Says: Do you believe you can count on him to return?

Duane: "Sure do. Don't be scared of Duane at all. There is no regret, because

I've yet to witness the same phenomenon. This is all I can say."

Sylvanus Then you feel like you're missing him. Do you think will he come back?

Duane: "He's not even missing. He knows where he is as I'm aware of where he is."

Sylvanus The Sylvanus: Do you have a clue where he's located?

Duane: "Basically, he's not even in the woods. They brought him in for whatever reason they decide to take them, and to conduct a few tests."

Sylvanus"Well what do you think you are?

Duane: "Not on this earth."

(Later in the interview later).)

Sylvanus The Sylvanus: Do you know you'll see him back?

Duane: "Sure do. It's a matter. People don't die."

Sylvanus You think you'll find him?

Duane: "Yeah, he'll be located and should he not return it's because the man wanted to stay."

It's a matter of taking the cat out of the bag. Duane states that the location of Travis is, and that Travis will be located two days before appearing again. Someone in Travis's family Travis Walton family or close family member would have been able to been able to let Duane know the events so that he wouldn't be in suffering over his loss. Travis.

These are the three key elements that seem to seal the lid on the particular case. There are numerous, many details about the incident, and much of it contradicts and contradictory. The most important thing I'd like to make is that this case is not like the stories that are featured on many TV documentaries that simply take the primary tale as a cut-and-dried, verified event that occurred exactly the way the lumbermen describe. The incident, just like that of the Betty and Barney Hill Incident which was made into a movie and book and later became part of the common Alien Abduction phenomenon. As a side note, it is interesting to note that the television movie made to promote Betty as well as Barney Hill aired on television on the 20th of

October, 1975, only 16 days prior to that incident. Travis Walton incident.

If a jury comprised of twelve individuals examined all of the available evidence,, would they conclude that the story in the case of Travis Walton was genuine or an elaborate hoax? If the jury consisted of skeptical skeptics, obviously they'd declare it a hoax, but in the case of a jury made of normal people I believe it's an unbalanced jury. That is, it will be difficult to convince twelve people to be able to decide one way or one way or the other. All evidence available to the subject does not go to an unambiguous proof of alien abduction however it provides a picture of largely circumstantial evidence that leads to a tilt in the story towards the brink of a fraud motivated by money. The reader is left to investigate these details and then make their own conclusions.

I believe that the Travis Walton case is similar to the anguish and pain the Betty or Barney Hill experienced. Travis Walton and the lumber men were both affected by a devastating and life-changing event. and he's a victim. The truth of the incident is in his mind, and that's the most important thing when it comes to your life's quality. It's only natural one would seek an amount of money to compensate for the psychological trauma suffered as a result of the incident and also the emotional turmoil that comes with dealing with it in the future, basically throughout his life.

Similar similar to similar to the Betty similar to the Betty Barney Hill case, the first view of the UFO is best kept distinct from the specific details about the abduction. The initial UFO view is genuine, however the abduction story could have been embellished inadvertently due to post-traumatic stress, hypnosis effects trauma or debilitating nightmares that resulted in altered memories of the incident.

The authenticity of the incident becomes less important when you realize that the participants are frequently victimized by the media and are often and require the help and support of their communities in order to return to their normal lives.

Chapter 8: More Troubles With Memories

"Dr. Susan Blackmore: "Now what we've learned about the method by which memory is formed is that the more you tell a story , the more likely you are to recall the story you told instead of the actual event. In the extreme this could be termed false memory. In this case, the memory may feel real and authentic, yet it was created by your own interpretation of the tale."

So, are abductees truly hearing what they are saying or is things up? Leah Haley claims she was taken several times by her family at Gulf Breeze, Florida, and later taken to what she claims to be an unidentified space craft. She has written several books about the subject and currently gives lectures on abductions by aliens all over the world. Though those memories from the incident were only recovered through the influence of hypnosis, she believes the event actually happened to her.

Leah Haley: "I didn't recall the whole incident, but I do recall being in a circular room that was filled with a bright, intense light and I lay on a platform that was flat on my back. I could see aliens all around me, performing tests on my body. They had black eyes that were solid with two small holes in their nose. I don't think I remember any mouth They didn't have hair, and they did not have ears. And I can remember feeling very serene, and not worried in the least. However, it felt like I was completely paralyzed. I couldn't get up and move. I felt like a medical professional."

Like many abductees Leah was a target of ridicule and rejection from her family and friends after her public disclosure. However, she stands by her story and campaign for this issue to be considered serious.

Leah Haley: "I got dismissed from a job I enjoyed because I believed it was necessary to share my story. My daughter, aged 24 rejected me after I went to the public in my personal story. She was married in July. I was not invited to her wedding. I was advised by my own daughter that she was never going to speak to me ever again. She didn't want to talk to me ever again. In her eyes, concerned I was dead, because I had embarrased the family by revealing the experiences I had."

In a bid to prove she was honest In order to prove her innocence, she consented to an ex- FBI profiler, Paul Minor, to conduct a thorough polygraph test on her.

Paul Minor: "I was an examiner of polygraphs for the Army up to 1978. Then, in 1978, I was transferred into the FBI and was the main polygraph examiner of the FBI from 1978 to about 1987 at which point I quit and set up my own business that was a security firm located in Fairfax, Virginia. (video 4)

Paul Minor: Do you plan to be a liar to my test in any manner during the exam?"

Leah Haley: "No.

Paul Minor: "Do you claim that you were abducted by aliens?"

Leah Haley: "Yes!

Paul Minor: "Are you lying about being examined gynecologically by aliens on spacecrafts?"

Leah Haley: "No.

Paul Minor: "Are you concerned that you may fail the polygraph exam?"

Leah Haley: "Yes!

Leah Haley:

"It appeared very real, as real as consciousness, being here and speaking right now. It was extremely challenging for me to believe it was real. I tried to justify it as it was a dream. I asked myself: "How can aliens gain entry into my home? All windows and doors were locked. However, it was so convincing that I was forced to check each window and door, and convince myself that they were all locked.

The polygraph test is anxious and stressful to sit for the test because you don't know how well the machine is able to read the material. It's as if I believe I'm honest however, how can the machine determine whether I'm lying as well?"

Interviewer: What she is doing on the test, if she did well or failed.

Paul Minor: "It showed that she was deceitful and that's not just my opinion however, she was also deceived, but there's a software in the computer here, which was created at John Hopkins University and I evaluated the charts based on that , and it also says deception is strongly implied, the likelihood of deceit being higher than .99. This is almost certain.

Interviewer: There were any doubts that you had in your minds that she was trying to fool us?

Paul Minor: "No doubt that I have in my head."

Interviewer: There's not any evidence that she believes that it could not be the case for her?

Paul Minor: "No, the fact that she believed the story, it would be clear that she was lying. But it also showed that she doesn't believe it , and she is certain that this was not the case."

Prof. Chris French (Psychologist, University of London): "Certainly there have been instances when people have shared abductions that were full-blown witnesses from outside who were in the same room at the time , reported that physically , they hadn't been removed from the space. This means that the whole event took place inside their minds. If we can say that it can happen in certain circumstances I believe it is the responsibility of proof that falls placed on those making more convincing claims that individuals are actually being taken aboard by flying sources to prove that this is not the case in every case."

Another issue when it comes to memories is the fact that it's difficult to tell the possibility that a person's memories could be altered due to the incident itself or through the direct manipulation of an alien. This is an example of the case of a situation that was published on the 16th of October, 2013, but the event actually took place in 1964. In his report Mike Hyde gives details which provide a clear instance of inconsistent memories from eyewitnesses at the time of the incident:

Mike Hyde UFO Report:

"This incident is one I witnessed when I was a 6 years old child. We lived in 2008 at N. Sherman Boulevard. Grand Island, NE. The neighborhood was relatively modern at the time and, as compared to modern times it was located on the edge of several farms as well as rural. The main road that ran east-west is Capitol Ave. and one block to the south of that was State St. Young kids who lived in the area attended West Lawn Elementary (not the modern one, but the old one on State St. & Broadwell).

The above photo is the view from the north from N. Sherman which was directly in front of our home. There weren't many trees in the area because the neighborhood was modern. There were fewer houses. The majority of the houses on the right were not constructed until the year 1965/66. This meant that the view to the north was quite clear and wide all the way to Capitol.

On August 8th 1964, a large portion of kids from the neighborhood and me were playing on the streets. It was the usual stuff, riding bikes and playing Army or just moving around. Many parents were busy doing yard work and washing their cars etc. A typical hot and dry day here in Central Nebraska.

A speck of light floated across the sky, moving NW to SE in its route of flight. The object caught everyone's attention fairly quickly. It was enormous. It was much larger than an airship or similar craft. It was a bit overcast the day of the event however, you could clearly see it. It was black and was with the shape of an oval cylinder. It was red with a line running through the middle that was illuminated and seemed almost electrical in the natural world. I can remember smells of the ozone. As you would when you cut an electrical wire or lightning. On the bottom and slightly towards the side was a sort of opening, or maybe a light source which was extremely blue-white. It wasn't an actual beam, or something else but it certainly was not apparent that way. It leads me to believe there was an opening, as it appeared, only to disappear at least a few times. I can't recall any sound coming from it. However, there was a weird sound, like a hearing a ringing sound however it was extremely high frequency. It didn't cause any harm or any other thing but the sound was present.

The conversation was going on and my dad (who isn't able to recall it ever happening) believed it was an USAF aircraft. One of our neighbors my buddy David Phelps' grandfather thought that it might be something the Russians created to scare people. What was odd about this was that the more it was there the quieter everyone became and then they the conversation stopped completely. They gazed in awe. My friend David and a acquaintance, who was a woman called Polly put down their phones and looked at it. There was no conversation, and no one moved. I believe at some point similar things happened to me.

This is roughly what the object appeared to be. I'm guessing here however I think it was larger than one-quarter mile in length. It was massive.

I don't have any recollection of when the incident occurred and the Sunday dinner that was the following day. I don't know the events that transpired in that and time, but the following day, we were boarding my dad's Valiant and headed to my grandmother's residence at 4th Street.

A majority of the children who were there on the were there that day still have nightmares about the incident. They remember it occurred, but none the adults can remember anything about it. It's like the memories of their parents were erased. This haunts me for over 50 years. It was in full clarity as if it were daylight."

***

This amazing incident is important because it describes in detail an event in which memories are altered and altered in an odd way. We've all seen the 'Men-in Black comedies in which a ridiculous device is employed to erase memories, and all parodies aside. it is a regular phenomenon that occurs in close encounters with aliens which must be considered when considering the subject of alien abduction , or any other alien encounter, for that matter.

Chapter 9: Dreaming Of Aliens

After the airing of "The UFO Incident' on television in 1975 and the extensive coverage in the press on the Travis Walton incident over the next year, the amount of instances related to Alien Abduction exploded. The debate over whether alien abductions really exist has been raging for many years. For abductees, these events are terrifying and vivid incidents, with many involving physical contact with aliens and spacecraft. Some skeptics believe what they're really experiencing is a type of serious sleep disorder.

The Dr. Susan Blackmore (Psychologist at the University of Plymouth): "The more I learn abduction stories, especially those that occur in the night, while sleeping in the evening, while people sleep and asleep, the more I observe the similarities between this and sleep paralysis. Sleep paralysis is actually quite widespread. Around 30 percent of people suffer from it. When you're dreaming, you'll be in a state of paralysis, but it usually goes away in the time before you actually awake, and you're not aware of it. However, sometimes the process fails and you awake and are still in a state of paralysis.

The paralysis is often connected with buzzing or sounds of humming, sensations of floating around or being dragged away and shivering skin sensations because there's something moving through your skin. It's also overwhelming the entire experience with a feeling of being in a space, the feeling that someone else is in the room.

If it doesn't wear off and you're left with... If you aren't sure what it is, it can be quite scary. You can now see the numerous similarities between it and abductions by aliens. I believe that a large portion of reports of alien abductions are actually elaborations of the sleep disorder."

Yvonne Smith (Alien Abductee Researcher): "But we know for a fact that all abductees are asleep. They're also experiencing these things. Yes, there's sleep paralysis. And yes, when they're asleep, a some of it is sleep paralysis. If someone is lying in bed reading , and bright light enters the room, and they are paralyzed and cannot move and are unable to sense something is happening inside their room What is the best way to explain this? What is the best way to explain who are driving on the highway? They're not sleeping and are not always with their own and therefore they're not creating this story because they've witnesses."

Professor. David Jacobs (Temple University): "This (has always been regarded as) to be a bit amazing. This is the extreme of the margin. Some people claim that they've been kidnapped in the hands of aliens from another world. The evidence is (considered) an evidence prima facie of mental disorder and is for long years.

For the first 20 to thirty years following this phenomenon the only thing we did was attempt to find out the psychological and mental health reasons that could be the reason this is taking place. We must discover the root cause of it since it's clearly psychological in nature. It's not happening according to the way people have described it.

It's not psychological. It's also not psychiatric. It's taking place, I think generally, in according to the way people describe it. It is my opinion that what we're seeing in this case is a physiological process of exploiting one species for another."

It is also evident the fact that. Blackmore's theories or assumptions of explanation could only be used in cases that occurred when the people in question were in bed or asleep. The argument does not provide any reason for abductions which occur when driving down the road, walking through woods, or even within one's own bedroom.

On the other side, Michael Raduga is the director and founder of the OOBE (Out of Body Experience) Research Center. He has conducted studies on the campus of UCLA (University of California in Los Angeles) in relation to Alien Encounters in a dream similar to lucid dreams or dream states. He concludes:

"The majority of the subjects experienced at least one complete or partial experience of being out of body and some had multiple. Subjects who were conscious while in a dream were told to alter their "lucid vision" into an experience that was out of body through the return to the physical body to be separated from it.

The possibility that extraterrestrials and UFOs are often encountered deliberately in a controlled way and within a matter of days, confirms that these experiences are the result of our brain. This was the first study to prove an encounter with UFOs as well as extraterrestrials result from the human brain. The study also proved that alien contact isn't an indication of the existence of extraterrestrial civilizations, but more of a shaky mental state that people often fall into unintentionally."

Michael Raduga provides a fascinating free ebook download that explains the techniques to create out-of-body experiences, which Raduga calls "The Phase". At the time of this writing, it is available for free download at http://obe4u.com/files/the_phase.pdf

Contact him directly by email at obe4u@obe4u.com

In spite of the many claims of 'it's all in your head' the person must prove with a physical proof of being taken hostage by aliens. This is the reason why the media paid so much attention to the'star-map' of Betty Hill. Many believed that it was a real artifact of an alien civilisation. Let's take a look at several more cases that show Alien Abduction and then we will discuss the possibility of discovering alien artifacts.

Alien Abduction Case 1

In December 1985 the writer Whitley Strieber went through a terrifying abduction by aliens from his home located in Upstate, New York. He recounted his experiences in his bestseller, "Communion", which was later made into a major movie.

Whitley Strieber "I awakened aware of the possibility that something was terrible wrong, and when I woke up, I noticed these terrifying figures surrounding me. They were small stalky figures with dark blue and tall and a willowy kind of figure with large eyes with black lenses and a snout kind of a narrow face. I believed that I was in fact being an nightmare. I tried to get up, but I was unable to because I was awake. I... was suffocating with among other things an acupuncture needle stuck to my skull It flashed in my eye. It was truly frightening. Then I went to sleep."

The Dr. David Jacobs: "One of the things abductees have told me in the past is the bizarre stares where an alien is able to enter and look directly into their eyes for the distance of just a few inches, or even one inch, or even touch one's forehead.

What's happening is the fact that this alien connected to their optic nerve, and making use of the optic nerve as an neural pathway. In doing so they are able to go through the brain activating or stimulating the neural pathways they wish to. They can also get data, which means it could be said that they are able to look into abductee's memories, or see the things an abductee has been doing over the last few weeks or even months. They are able to use data to their advantage if they want as well as trigger emotional reactions for any procedure they wish to carry out They can manage the person however they wish."

What happened in the cabin is to be determined. Strieber claims that it was a true incident and not just a fantasy. In addition, he mentions that over the next four years, 19 other people claimed to have seen aliens in the exact same location.

Professor. Susan Blackmore gives a opposite view: "Alien abduction experiences could be a form of what's known as a'metachoric experience. This is a distinct type of auto-state of consciousness where it appears that you're within the world of normality and yet you've been hallucinating all things. The most popular instance of this is called"false awakenings. You dream that you've awakened. You're in a dream, you're dreaming that you wake up, maybe wake up and clean your teeth, go out the house, and everything seems perfectly normal , and then you realize that something isn't right in any way. "Oh my god I'm dreaming Then you awake."

Interviewer: What's the experience of recalling the event now, after many years?

Whitley Strieber "It appears as if it's occurring again. It's just as vivid as the day it took place. The memory will not fade for one second. It's in my brain. I can remember it well."

Nick Pope (Ministry of Defense): "I've met Whitley Strieber a few occasions and am convinced that he's completely honest regarding his experience. Whitley Strieber is certainly someone who has had an extraordinary experience. If it's extraterrestrial or non I'm not sure. I'm not certain that Whitley would define it this way. It's certainly alien because it's not related to our perception and I believe that Whitley and other people who are similar to him have had an experience that was quite remarkable."

The group of support featured in "Communion" was inspired by a real abduction support group led by Budd Hopkins in New York City, which has been meeting each week for the past 35 years.

Budd Hopkins (Abduction Counselor): "One of the questions that are often asked of abductees themselvesis "Why me? "

Everyone's "Why me?" and there's no solution for this. We don't have any idea. The only thing we know is that someone is experiencing abductions that they'll experience throughout their lifetime, they'll experience it repeatedly as being an involuntary sample in a person's long-term research. This person will eventually come to maturity and has children of their own. It is very likely that one or several of these children will be taken away. It's like aliens are following a certain genetic lineage."

Every Friday night, about 10 people meet at Hopkins"midtown" house to discuss their stories. Many find it a necessary way of coping through the trauma.

Peter Robbins (Abduction Researcher): "What I feel is taking place at the root of abduction is that a different intelligence, whether from the present or another location is forcibly interfacing with humans. I believe it's against their wishes in an array of pre-planned or experiments, initially. Then, a sequence of methods that point to an extremely disturbing scenario and that is, we're being misled by."

Alien Abduction Case 2

The most shocking abduction cases Hopkins examined took place in the month of November at New York City to a woman whose name was Linda Napolitano; she originally wanted to remain anonymous and used an alias Linda Cortile.

Linda: "Well, on November 30 1989, I went to sleep and noticed this numbness creeping upwards from my toes into my legs and I could feel there was a presence within the room. And I was frightened to open my eyes and for some time, but later I was forced to do so for the sake of protecting myself and my family, and when I sat up, there was this thing, that thing was standing on my mattress. It was large and had eyes and black eyes. It was a shade of gray and wasn't right there. I was scared. I thought I going to have an attack of the heart, I'll be truthful with you. I was afraid I'd go to heart failure. It was exactly how I felt."

Linda was placed in contact with Budd Hopkins, who performed several Hypnotic regressions. These sessions revealed a variety of mysterious details about the abduction.

Linda: "Well, I discovered myself in the window, twelve stories up in the air and could not breathe. It was very difficult to breathe. It felt like my eyes were stuck in their sockets. They did not move, and the only thing I did was stare at the sky. I was bathed in a blueish white light that was a bit smokey, and that's the only thing I could see. The second thing I remembered was that I felt like I was in an invisible elevator that was going through this space and back. Then I was taken to this room with a very clinical appearance in which I was dressed and sitting on a table. It was possible that there were around four or five creatures. They then began to study me."

Budd Hopkins "One aspect concerning this subject is that when you witness something that is dramatic or discover something by reading or otherwise One thing that you immediately realize that, if this's real, it's the most significant human event ever. If indeed there's an intelligent being that's not human, employing some sort of non-human technology that is now interacting with humans, it's a major ever human event. I can't imagine coming across this without being incredibly intrigued and ready to study the possibility of it."

According to the people who investigated the abduction, there were numerous witnesses who witnessed UFOs hovering above the area where the incident took place.

Yvonne Smith (Abduction Researcher) The witnesses observed the craft hovering above her apartment. When Budd displays the drawings of witnesses from different angles, it's astonishing and the main thing we must to communicate to the general public. It's that these individuals aren't being abducted by themselves in some field. This could happen anywhere."

Budd Hopkins (Abduction Counselor): "I have looked through about 620 different individuals. And I've had numerous meetings with some of those individuals... In many of these instances, I went through perhaps five, six, seven, or eight 10 abduction stories. I've had the opportunity to speak with another 4000 individuals via letters or phone, faces-to-face, or descriptions they gave me, but I did not have the opportunity to follow up with them. However, the numbers are astonishing."

The Dr. David Jacobs: "What people have said is that they are taken outside their home regardless of whether they're sitting on their sofa or in the their kitchen, or wherever else they are , and most of the time they're taken away through a window that is closed. I've asked them, 'Are you certain about this? that it's closed? did you actually open it? did you open it? did they open it by themselves? and the abductees have said "No, it's completely closed. However, if it was a psychological issue and they were able to say "Of course it's open'. It shouldn't be a problem so. However, they look at me and ask "Has anyone else had this happen? It's floating through a closed window And they don't realize that everyone reports it."

Interviewer: What do you say if this wasn't for you? In the neighborhood with people you know If you'd heard that this was the case for somebody else. What would you think? What reaction would you have?

Linda: "I'd probably would not believed it. I'd be extremely skeptical. And I'd expect the majority of people will feel the same way about my situation. However, I am aware of what happened to me."

One of the main problems that skeptical people face with the authenticity of Linda's abduction and the entire phenomenon generally involved the use of the hypnotic technique in order to help her recall the incident. The argument is that this allows for alteration of the person, and in certain cases, the actual creating of an abduction experience.

The Dr. Susan Blackmore (Psychologist) is still unconvinced: "Imagine someone has had an extremely traumatizing sleep paralysis experience. Imagine that they woke up during the dark, could not move, could not scream or scream, and they felt creepy crawly hands on their bodies, felt the sensation of being surrounded by someone in the room, heard humming and buzzing noises and then , later, they awoke and it's all gone. What will they be thinking?

Imagine going to a hypnotherapist. She goes back in time and says "You're able to remember, you'll remember, you're lying in mattress, the sounds are present, you're able to recall. It's a good thing we are aware that hypnosis can stimulate fantasy and it is common for people to fantasize. It is likely that they'll think about aliens, specifically in the case of a hypnotherapist who is well-known for his alien regressions of abduction. So, this dream, they'll be aware that it's not real because that's what the hypnotherapy process is normally used to create. However, it slowly gets into their minds. It's only necessary to go through that process a couple of times before your memories have been able to be vivid, vivid and completely convincing. You know for certain that you've been abducted. In reality you were not."

Budd Hopkins "Hypnosis Naturally is the whipping-boy of skeptical because it's utilized often in this way. Hypnosis can often be misused. If an extremely intelligent interrogator can guide someone to a conversation that is normal to be hypnotized, it's quite possible, if we take a look at lawyers in action for example, but even during a regular conversation people could be led to be enticed, lured, altered, nearly against their will, and the story changes. When hypnosis is used, it's much simpler to achieve this."

Alien Abduction Case 3

We now come to the case of a person who isn't widely known by the public at large. the film was not made about it. The people involved did not seek fame or fortune out of their experience however it remains among the top shocking instances that has ever been recorded. Alien Abduction ever recorded.

The incident occurred along the banks of the Pascagoula River on the 11th of October in 1973. Charles Hickson and Calvin Parker had planned to go out for an evening of fishing, but they landed something that was way beyond their wildest dreams. The interview was recorded in 1987:

Charles Hickson and Calvin Parker

Charles Hickson "I believe I won't ever forget what happened and of course, it happened on the 11th of October, 1973. It was my job at FB Walter & Son Shipyard at the time. Calvin was also one of my friends. In the evenings, after work, I'd go for a fishing trip in the river whenever I had time. That the day was particularly noon, Calvin and myself had planned to go fishing the evening after work.

After we'd gone home and gotten our gear and then we set off down the river. We tried numerous spots before coming back to the former shipyard. I'm not certain what ...,what was the thing that caught my attention, but I did hear the sound of a hissing sound. when I turned to look in the direction of my gaze, there was something, a craft. It was likely 18 inches or one foot above the ground, just sitting there. There were two blue lights in the front and they were either spinning or vibrating. I was unsure what to make of it; I wasn't sure the cause, and it was a shock to me at first. I stepped from the pier and glanced around, and I saw Calvin also stepping down and was doing the same thing as me when we got down the door that was opened to the front. it appeared to be to be it was a sliding door.

A brilliant light that came from outside the craft, simply a bright beam of light. There was something else that, well , I'm pretty sure that it was robots However, there was something that walked into the door. There were three in all, one was even behind the other and they seemed to move out of the door. They never even touched the ground. I wasn't sure which way to go, and I'm terrified at that moment as the river was in front of us, and we can't travel that way, so it were coming closer to us.

When they came up close to me, I just stopped, I do not know. Then they came back and one took the other arm, which I was able to feel pain in a flash and one of them grabbed control of the other arm. It was like I just rose above the ground, to the point they were in , more or less leaning towards me.

They weren't particularly tall, I'm 5' eight inches tall and was a bit higher that they. Around that date, Calvin, he was on my right. I observed one taking his hand and he went limp. Later, I learned that he was passing out. He fainted because of the fear , I believe. Whatever took place, and we walked into the cabin through the door, and then the bright light reflected into what was probably the center of a compartment or room; it seemed to me to be round , and the light was shining off the ceiling and walls, and even the floor.

We stopped around mid-way through the room, I believe and they released me. I could not move anything except my eyes. I was able to move my eyes but I don't know how I was able to move them but nothing else. However, they let me go and for a couple of minutes I'm guessing it was, however, directly in front of my face something emerged from the wall. It was to me as an enormous, and I've always thought it was an eye, a large pupil and an eye. It moved to my face, and remained there for a few minutes perhaps minutes, and then it fell down and under me. I'm guessing that it was up the back because it re-emerged over my head. It then came again in front of me and continued to be there for a couple of minutes additional minutes, possibly one or two minutes or so. It then moved back into the wall's light and vanished."

I was suspended indefinitely I wasn't sure what to do what I could do. I kept thinking about what would they take me? Will they remove me or I didn't know what they would be doing or even what were up to with me. However, after a few minutes the things returned and grabbed me, and I felt like we were about to be turning around in the room, and then we went back to the entrance and then back to almost the exact spot they picked me up from. They then let go of me, and my body fell on the floor.

Then it was time that I was able to see Calvin again . He was stood on the bank of the river, arms extended and appeared to be in shock. I was trying to get on my feet and make an effort to talk to him and see whether I could assist him in somehow, when I heard that sound once more and then I glanced at the back of me and saw the blue lights quickly and this boat disappeared.

Then I got towards Calvin and was standing at this point, and it took me a while to reach him in a position where I could speak to the man and assure him perhaps it was because we weren't seriously hurt I'm sure, but we weren't aware of what they'd committed to us.

At first , we thought we would not tell anyone about it and would be quiet about it since I didn't want being labeled a crazy or a nut and such things are not meant to occur. However, the more I thought about it, more I realized we'd need to inform someone, possibly the military as we know that our country might pose an imminent threat to our nation.

When we got to the stop on our way back I called Keesler Air Force Base from Payphone and briefly trying to convey the situation, however they informed me that they couldn't manage these things, and they said we'd have to deal with police at the sheriff's station in our area.

We hesitated because we didn't want contact the sheriff's department since, you know, they might just pick us and drag us to the nuts' house. We discussed about it again and decided to contact the sheriff's department , and perhaps we could ask the department to guarantee us that there wouldn't be any media attention about the incident.

So I contacted the sheriff's office and they sent two deputies to the scene who after speaking to us we were asked to go to the sheriff's office and we did. They questioned us for a long time, and the sheriff told me that at night that we would not receive any publicity whatsoever about the incident He might even consider bringing it to the appropriate authorities. Regardless of who the appropriate authorities were, the matter could be investigated.

The next day, as we arrived at work, my phone rang and it was a report from Jackson and the phone lines at the shipyard began to ring. The crew was trying to obtain details about what occurred to Charlie Hickson and Calvin Parker last night in Pascagoula.

Overall I believe that the general public has been a great source of support to me. I've never been the subject of ridicule throughout my life; I think it's because I've been honest , and when people wanted to ask questions regarding it, I devoted my time to answer their questions.

Sometimes, I am thinking that maybe I shouldn't have revealed to anyone about what occurred to me on the Pascagoula river several years ago. But then I am reminded that I was right in sharing what happened. I believe that the majority of people are aware of the places man has been. I believe I know where we're heading; perhaps one day I'll be able to convince people of that truth. I am sure there are other universes with life and all of us will be able to recognize that it's a fact without a doubt.

Later in life, Charles Hickson made these remarks:

"There must be an existence out there I'm not sure the exact location, but there must be a place where they originate from.

***

Although it isn't as well-known in the same way as Betty or Barney Hill case or the Travis Walton Case, this incident was also targeted from Philip Klass. Both men passed the polygraph test, however Philip Klass claimed the examiner was not experienced. Other people have expressed the possibility that Calvin Parker changed his story in the years following his death; that later he claimed that the polygraph was not passed out, but had bizarre experiences aboard the vessel.

Charles Hickson passed away in 2011 at age 80. He did not alter his story. In spite of the critics and the negative criticisms from skeptical individuals The Pascagoula Incident is one of the most convincing cases I've come across in the field of Alien Abduction.

The day of the incident, Hickson Parker and Hickson Parker were interrogated with the

Sheriff of their local area. they used a clever trick to the pair. They left them in the police station, in the room with an unintentional tape recorder. They believed that they could quickly be able to tell the truth about an elaborate ploy by listening on their private conversations. The tape showed that the men were in a real state of shock and dismay over what they had experienced. This is a fragment of the transcription of the recording:

Calvin Parker: I almost was a victim of a heart attack. I'm not shitting you. I was one millimeter away from dying.

Charlie Hickson: I'm sure that this scared me to death as well. Jesus...have mercy.

Calvin Parker: I was in tears I could not help it. The worst part is that no one will believe in us.

Charlie Hickson: I'm sure of that, and I can't bear all that. I thought I'd gone through enough misery on this Earth but now I had to endure this.

Calvin Then I'll tell you that I'm supposed to take some pills or see an ophthalmologist or something. I'm unable to take it anymore I'm going to get crazy.

CharllE: I'll tell you, once we've finished I'll give you something to help you settle down , so you can finally get some restful sleep.

CALVIN: I'm not able to get to sleep, even though it's already midnight. I'm pretty sure I'm crazy.

Charlie Then, Calvin, when they took you out, when they got me out of the thing Goddamn it, I would do not want to ever have you straightened up.

CALVIN: My arms I remember that they all froze up and I was unable to move. Like when I fell on a rattlesnake.

The CHARLIE: They did not treat me this way.

CALVIN"I passed out. I'm sure I've never was able to sleep in my entire life.

CharllE: I've not had anything like it before in my entire life. It's impossible to convince people of.

CALVIN CALVIN: I don't wish to sit here forever. I'd like to see an ophthalmologist.

Charlie: They should awaken and believe... the need to begin to believe.

CALVIN: Can you can see how the door came right up?

The CHARLIE: I'm not sure how it got opened, son. I'm not sure.

CALVIN: It laid down and like the son's twitches, just like they do when they are out.

Charlie: I'm sure. You can't believe it. It's impossible to convince people to believe it.

CALVIN: I was paralyzed immediately. I was unable to move.

CHARLIE: They'll never believe it. They'll be believing it at some point. It could be too to late. I've always known they were from different universes. I've known all along. I had no idea that it would happen to me.

CALVIN: You're a good person. I don't drink.

CHARLIE: I'm sure of this, my son. When I arrive at the house, I'm going to buy me another drink and then make me fall asleep. See, what are we sat around looking for. I need to talk to Blanche... What are is it that we've been are we

CALVIN: I have to go home. I'm getting sick. I need to get out from here.

CALVIN: It's difficult to believe . . . Oh my God, this is awful... I'm sure there's a God in the heavens.

The next day following that incident Hickson along with Parker was interviewed by military personnel in Keesler Air Force Base at the time it was discovered that other witnesses had also seen UFOs in the same area incident, corroborating their account. This included one Parole Officer who went named Raymond Broadus.

The MUFO journal dating from 1984 has published an account of the military interview which is found within Appendix 3. The military didn't want to make public this transcript, and it is interesting to observe how it is consistent and eyewitness reports from the local parole office as well as the attendant at the gas station.

Charlie Hickson always said he believed he was conscious throughout the entire experience, but the actor also admitted that he could be lost in consciousness because the fact that he did not remember ever leaving the ship but more of the moment he stepped back in the open. The Pascagoula incident is still one of the most convincing cases in the field of Alien Abduction to this day.

Chapter 10: Communication Posted

in Northern Wisconsin in 1975, Karen Klinger and Dennis Muraskwa were enjoying a vacation with their family in 1975 when the pair decided to take a walks together. They saw something interesting out of the blue sky.

Karen Klinger: "We saw an orange-colored bright star just above the horizon of the trees that were on the other part of the lake. And it then zipped towards at the peak of our heads."

Dennis Muraska: "I thought you could define the flight as dragonflies. The fly would zip and stop , then zip here and then stop; Zip, zip and zip very fast. I thought, 'what are the people watching?' began to call my parents to the cabin to see the show and my mother was a bit worried."

Karen Klinger: "Dennis sister's boyfriend entered the house, grabbed an enormous beam flashlight , and used it for flashing UFOs. UFO 3 times. They disappeared instantly. Then, perhaps two seconds later, they flashed at us in the same amount of times we been flashing at them."

Dennis Muraska: "By this time , we realized we were being watched by something we didn't know the reason for and it was quite bizarre and certainly appeared to be cleverly controlled."

Following an incident Muraska as well as Klinger felt dizzy and sick. When they later discussed the incident, they realized that they were unable to remember the duration of the night.

Dennis Muraska: "At one moment, we looked upwards and saw the moon directly aligned with the rear view mirrors of the vehicle. By the time we returned to the lake, which shouldn't have taken too long the moon was already setting."

Karen Klinger: "It never ever occurred to me until that point that there might be a gap in time. As soon as I realized I felt sick, and I felt sick at the thought of it."

To find more answers, Dennis and Karen each were hypnotized.

Dennis Muraska: "We compared notes and later they agreed extremely closely the suggestions that Karen made under her. We purchased these photos of grids-like patterns."

The obvious goal of the abduction of their victims was to force the people who were touched into the bearer of a message"The Earth is linked with the rest of the world.'

Karen Klinger: "If you think this been your experience then take whatever steps you can to discover the truth as it's well worth the risk."

***

Another person whom claims that he received messages through abductions has been identified as Steve Neill. He claims that aliens have warned him of the need for humankind to be helped. requires help.

Steve Neill: "We've separated our self from nature. We are of the belief that nature's out there, and we're here. Nature was created for us to be able to do whatever we want, and to throw away nature in the name of personal gain or profits. I'm convinced we're at risk of becoming extinct just like dinosaurs."

In many of his abductions Neill has been shown terrifying images of the future.

"They bring me into the scene, no matter if you've seen the world following the nuclear war. They transport me through the streets, and I can observe all the bodies and all the debris. I am aware that they're trying to convey me a message that you have heard of and I'm required to receive this message of this potential future and act upon it , and then try to convey it to the world."

For others, similar visions have prompted them to create or join groups of support. Many believe that the messages or images received from aliens are an indication that humans can alter their fate.

Alien Artifacts

It is possible that an abducted person returned with a physical object from their encounter with an alien that would be evidence of the fact that their abduction experience was authentic. A doctor believes that he has this evidence. His surname is Dr. Roger Leir. Here are some evidence-based details concerning his work:

Dr. Roger Leir is a surgeon from Southern California who has been operating on patients for more than thirty years.

The Dr. Roger Leir: "So far 8 surgeries were carried out and through the eight surgeries, we've taken out nine things. The main thing that is common is that everyone are victims of the phenomenon of alien abduction."

In 1996, he undertook one of his first procedures to remove an implant in the jaw of the abductee.

Doctor. Roger Leir: "The man we performed the procedure on, to perform the procedure of removing any object that was in the jaw left was in private business and had a background of abductions by aliens."

As with the majority of abductees the patient was hesitant to reveal his identity or show his face publicly.

The Dr. Roger Leir: "There is a certain stigma associated with abductees. They have an inherent fear of telling someone about what transpired. They may be worried that they'll lose their job, or that their career could be at risk and even lose money, and there are a lot of practical aspects to be aware of.

Doctor. Leir describes some of the amazing findings that were discovered in this remarkable procedure: "There is no portal to enter the body; there is no proof of how the object entered the body. After we examined tissues surrounding the object, we observed that there was not an inflammation; this cannot be true because anything that enters the body is likely to trigger an inflammatory response. Thirdly, they are surrounded by a vast variety of neuroproprioceptors, which aren't the correct anatomy.

When the outer biological membrane was removed and revealed the triangular-shaped object. the object was encased within a gray membrane. Interestingly, this membrane couldn't be cut, even using the surgical scalpel.

Close-up image of an alien implant

The implant was then shipped to the Los Alamos National Laboratory for testing of the metallurgical properties.

Dr. Leir: "We knew that when we received the initial report of Los Alamos that we didn't have anything in common due to the fact that Los Alamos is a world top laboratory and they would never recommend further testing of any thing they felt odd. It was therefore the mix of the elements present in the objects which motivated them to recommend to conduct more tests."

The implant was later sent into New Mexico Tech Laboratory which was where various tests of metallurgical strength were carried out on the object.

Dr. Leir: The theory that they proposed was that they were fragments of meteorites. They didn't know they were taken from the human body.

The New Mexico Tech lab report discovered that the components inside the implant were made of meteorites, which are so rare, only a few had been identified. In this stage the scanning electron microscope examination was carried out to examine the device. The results showed that the implants were made and not natural meteorites. Tests revealed that implants were connected to nerve endings of the patient.

Dr. Leir: "The second set of tests that followed a number of the tests conducted at New Mexico was run by University of California at San Diego."

The results of the laboratory at UCSD confirmed earlier studies The majority of the metal that was analyzed within the device was exoterrestrial, and did not originate from Earth.

Dr. Leir: "Some of the elements found together were non-terrestrial in source, extra-terrestrial, or alien origins.

There is a lot of evidence, and the implications are incredible. In every instance the evidence chain is documented and the test results are shocking.

Professor. Leir: This could be the evidence that scientists have been searching for. The implications of this discovery go all over the world and impact every living being.

***

Of course, Dr. Leir is not without his critics. Penn & Teller did a critical blurb about the work he has done in one their HBO videos, and there are numerous reviews that question his work. Should the Dr. Leir could get additional evidence from medical professionals or could persuade any of his patients speak openly about the circumstances that led to how the procedure was carried out, that will add importance to the evidence that he has presented.

A Global Phenomenon

While the majority of reports on abductions come directly from United States, it is actually a global phenomenon with thousands of instances being reported within the United Kingdom alone. The person in charge of investigating these reports for the UK government, was Nick Pope.

Nick Pope: "Whilst it's accurate to say that various governments have conducted studies into UFOs that have mirrored the work I conducted at the ministry. However, to my knowledge I am the only person in the world to conduct official investigation and research into the phenomenon of alien abduction.

I was asked by a few people while I was working in the ministry: Why are you spending your time researching alien abductions?' told them that so long as they have the courage to tell me about these experiences I have a responsibility to investigate their claims. A few of them were calling me in complete dismay. What do I do? Do I hang up on them?"

A case he was involved in is Peter as well as Diane Shepard, who saw an enormous, brightly lit UFO from their home in the countryside.

Diane Shepard: "There, right in front of us along the highway, which was the main road there were some of the most incredible light show on the sky on our left. There were a lot of them, and they actually came from our left side, crossing the road, and after that they came in the front of us, and heading toward the right."

Peter Shepard: "This was an entire field, from the field, by the way. The lights were at treetop height but the reds, there was the effect of a high-low of sparkling, flashing brilliant white flashes being released."

Diane Shepard: "We were amazed by the things we saw. Our world was completely destroyed. It was not expected to happen."

Peter Shepard: "How can you explain something like that... you're sure... How can this happen? This is an amazing experience. You can't believe it. I was ecstatic and a bit scared slightly uneasy due to the sheer dimensions of this beast. It was incredible."

Professor. Chris French: "The essence of the experience is not something I would dispute. It was often apparent to the person who was experiencing it to be taking place in the manner they described it. The issue is how do we interpret what transpired. Could they have had an extremely rich and complex hallucination that was the reason they were experiencing it?"

Another intriguing instance occurred Ann Paul and Paul Andrews, whose son, Jason, was repeatedly visited by UFOs throughout his early years. Every time the house began to shake violently and a flash of light appeared through the windows and doors and Jason would walk towards the front door before heading out into their backyard. Jason would go missing for hours at a time.

Ann Andrews: "I mean that the first reaction is pure terror. You're walking around like an un-headless chicken. You're not sure if you need to call police, or even what you should do. You're standing there, you know you're screaming at one another. The other response is anger. You realize that real anger is possible. What's the point of doing something to stop it? This is like the time when Jason was younger. He would call us and say , 'I'm angry at the fact that they took me, however, I am angry at the fact that you didn't stop them. You're extremely upset. You're very upset. Also, you are unhappy that it's happening kind of at your home, your personal home, where you're supposed to safeguard your children and ensure their safety and do nothing to change it."

Nick Pope: "Some people have thought that the issue we're discussing when we talk about the grays, could be the human race's future evolution into. There has been speculation that we're dealing with future-looking people returning through time to acquire genetic material possibly to revive humanity."

Ann Andrews: "He told us that that was the thing that happened to him. It was true that he had repeatedly told us that he was taken away by small men. It was around the time he was about four or five years old. He told me that these little boys visit my room, and force me to leave with them'. We replied that no one can enter the door, the doors are closed, daddy and mommy are there to guard you. All the things parents say. It was he who was insisting that this was what was happening."

Paul Andrews: "I'd like to know the reason. If you could stop it, then I'd do my best to stop it."

Nick Pope (investigator at UK Ministry of Defence): "At the end of the day, my greatest conclusion, and since this is a an opinion I developed within the ministry, what you could say that an official opinion and that is that we're dealing in extraterrestrials, and that the phenomenon of alien abduction is physical in nature."

So what's going on? Do thousands being taken from their homes at wishes by aliens? Are sinister experiments conducted on the human race by spacecrafts?

Perhaps the most innovative interpretation of the phenomenon comes by Budden, the British science researcher Albert Budden. He spent a long time researching the theory that alien abductions don't exist as physical phenomena, but rather are mental reactions triggered by exposure to extreme levels electrical energy. It is interesting to note that only a small proportion of people are able to feel a heightened reaction from this phenomenon, which results in vivid and life-like hallucinations.

Albert Budden: "All these abductees and experiences are being affected by a condition known as electrical hypersensitivity. The word "hypersensitivity" indicates that they are highly sensitive to invisible electromagnetic energy within the surrounding environment. They reside in hotspots, in which the electromagnetic energies are greater than in most locations. There are power lines near and radio transmitters and over a crack in the earth that can be described as a fault in the geology that creates electromagnetic fields. A transformer is located near the transformer. are a variety of electromagnetic sources within the surrounding environment. It is an individual source. There are many types of this such as a radio ham next door, or a CP radio fan a a few meters away. These things can emit a home in a continuous manner."

According to Button's study the experiences experienced by abductees mirror the experiences of those who are afflicted by powerful electromagnetic currents.

"They are prone to experiencing periods of time when they believe that there's an individual within the room looking at them, even though they don't see anyone and they refer to it as the feeling of being in a room. Their perception of time may be altered, this is known as the feeling of desynchronisation in which they feel as if the time has passed by quickly or that the time has been altered or dragged out. There are a myriad of symptoms and signs that they be afflicted with after exposure to excessive amounts of electrical magnetic."

Budden's theory is unable to provide a reason for how two people (Like in the instance of Paul Andrews and Ann Andrews) could experience the same "hallucination" - this explanation for such a situation seems to be a bit unlikely.

Also, are alien abductions really real? Are people being transported into spaceships and subjected strange experiments? Are these an extreme mental disorder? The abductees themselves are convinced that this is an actual thing. Yet the physical evidence is extremely thin to virtually inexistent.

In the end of the day, this is a phenomenon that is believed to affect millions of people all over the globe. In the meantime, until we can determine the real cause the abduction files will be open.

Budd Hopkins "The primary reason is that UFO's inhabitants have reached an technological dead-end, which is an assumption, but I believe it's a pretty safe assumption. It is also believed that they must revive their own stocks by acquiring something, perhaps something that is more primitive than anything we could offer which they appear to require. This is an initiative for them and not us. We don't know the direction this program is expected to take us. However, many have shared stories of encounters on ships, and in the experience, characters that appear to be a mixture of human and alien features."

Dr. Susan Blackmore: "In my opinion, in the end, is that the majority of abductions by aliens actually occur in sleep paralysis. The fact that people have awoken being paralyzed from dreams. They're half asleep and can't move. they show all the typical symptoms of sleep paralysis , such as buzzing and humming, bright light and the sensation of being in the presence of someone else and then their mind takes over and takes care of all the rest. They dress everything in the gear of an extraterrestrial abduction."

Nick Pope: "The biggest issue with research on alien abduction in the present is that with the greatest intentions in the world, it's been conducted by a few dedicated amateurs. The only way to advance research into this vital issue requires the support of the mainstream scientific community as well as the involvement of the government. Only these two entities which I believe can move this issue forward and possibly be able to make some breakthroughs."

Leah Haley: "Abduction is terrifying Abduction is terrifying but the viewers must be aware that these events are real, physical events have occurred for millions and I wouldn't be surprised if someone I have met is an abductee however, they've never mentioned that they were abducted."

Chapter 11: Is Alien Abduction True Or

False?

There are some of us who are convinced that we are not the sole person within the Universe. There is a strong belief that aliens are real. This is further exacerbated by the fact that unidentified flying objects are soaring around the planet without being recognized by the most advanced radar systems. Some consider that many of those who were captured are at large , and are protected by some of the largest countries around the globe. The situation is further aggravated because of those that believe aliens may be able to kidnap humans without our knowledge or capability to stop them.

It's true, there are groups and movements founded with the sole purpose of helping people who have been taken by foreigners. There are theories or actual facts used to lead the defense of individuals from these crimes. If you've ever been a victim of one, then you'll probably know the motives behind the need to keep this information on hand. If that is the case, then there has to be a way to determine if the person was abducted from an unknown source.

Anyone can be abducted nearly everywhere. There are some places where aliens are known to love taking us by surprise , especially when we're unable to move or are in a state of isolation. If you've experienced an encounter with them, then you will likely know the most effective ways to make this method can work. If you've never had a contact with them, then you may be thinking about whether this is true. While you wait for the day you'll be convinced, you need to take your time to figure out the right way to know whether you've been kidnapped or just confusion in your brain.

There are some who believe that loved ones of theirs were abducted by aliens or have disappeared and not been found. Some who have been taken captive have been able to return but have an unwritten set of rules of conduct, which form the foundation of the argument that aliens are real and are able to abduct , capture and even kill people with no knowledge. There are some who believe that aliens have the ability to communicate with them when there is something they require. Some believe that they test them prior to releasing them.

Whatever the case, we must be aware of these creatures if they actually exist since we aren't sure if they are genuinely trying to help or cause harm to humanity. So, when you lie down at night or when you drive , you must be extremely aware of the direction you're going along with the time and keep an eye on your surroundings. This article will discuss ways to tell that you've been taken by an extraterrestrial. It is important to know if you're close to being captured and if you don't be aware, you might have been abducted before and then released by aliens.

6 Features Of Alien Abduction While You Are Asleep

The most ideal time for someone to target you is when you're in a state of sleep. In the case of aliens, this could be the ideal time to kidnap humans and transport them or her to places you would never be able to reach when you were awake. For majority of people, this might sound like a dream, however, there are some who are convinced that they have been captured by aliens. If not, how do you explain why you awake at midnight and do things or go to places you've never been to? The most effective way to determine whether you've been snatched by aliens when you're asleep is to do a search on the following elements.

Strange Noises Before You Go to Sleep

What number of times do you have heard noises in your bedroom before going to bed? Then you feel a sense of sleepiness whenever you hear the same. Many people ignore this occurrence, thinking it's normal. However, one thing you must be aware of is that when you are unable to describe a specific behavior you feel or that isn't possible under normal circumstances, it might be that aliens are trying to bring you along with them. Keep an eye out!

The Dreaming Of Aliens

Have you taken the time to reflect on the events that occur in the dream you just had? Many people do not think about this. A few people do not even realize that they were captured by"aliens" as they fell asleep and performed mentally implantation of the forms that they forget because they seldom see them. Have you ever dreamed of beings that are difficult to comprehend. Perhaps you've seen flying objects you can't remember when you awake early in the day. If these are the things you see in your dreams then you must look for the eyes of the beings who took you captive. If they do, then you've been taken by aliens!

The feeling of watching someone else You

If you are feeling in the night before bed that someone is watching you, then be sure that you are in the right place and that someone is watching you. If this person watching you is not identifiable and you are unsure, then you should believe that someone else is present. This is further exacerbated by the possibility that you awake in the late at night and think that someone is in the world watching you. You may find some shadow or an object that is that is looking directly at you while you lay in bed. Which person do you suppose they are? If you know an answer to this question, please share.

Sleep Walking

Many people believe that if you slept in one location and then you ended up in another, it is a normal thing to do. However, this isn't always the scenario. Some people believe that the majority are those who have consumed large amounts of alcohol and are unable to fully comprehend their are asleep. How then do explain that you didn't drink any alcohol, and then ended up in a different place?

You Feel Paralyzed

Have you identified the reasons you feel a bit numb the moment you awake in the morning, or after a long sleep? Perhaps you've no idea that this is normal. On the contrary, it is a very powerful persona that is portrayed by those who display evidence of aliens abducting people.

You may see some blood on your Beddings

Another method can signal that you've encountered the aliens and are an abductee. If you don't have an explanation for the bloody drips that you see on your bedding when you awake in the morning, then you ought to blame it on the alien that came to visit you during the middle of the night when you fell in bed. Maybe the alien collected an unspecified amount of blood to test the experiments you've pictured being carried out on you.

3 Signs of Alien Abduction While driving

There are a myriad of things you may get into while you drive. Many of these problems people overlook because they don't have a straightforward explanation that is reasonable to give. If you could be a person of integrity and provide all the details required, you will be able to discover the actual evidence that other species exist on this world. If you are unable to tell the nature of the events you encounter, then believe that aliens were the main factor in the events you are currently in. If this information was closely examined, then there is a massive awareness of the presence of aliens.

Unexpected Breakdown

There are situations where you encounter strange objects while driving. There are ones that you can't discern. If they're flying you ought to be wary of these objects. Most times, when you've spotted these things, you have discovered that your car has a breakdown. The breakdown isn't an ordinary event, but it's quite rapid. You are unable to describe what has occurred to your car, after seeing the flying objects unidentified.

Unknown Movements Following Pull Over

How often have you had to stop while driving? It could be to investigate something you noticed or simply to pay attention to something. What you experience or feel afterward could be the impression of being a stranger. When you stop on your vehicle, you discover you driving on the same road again, without clue as to the way you got back into the vehicle. You may have also encountered a car breakdown after driving for a while. After a short time , your car is running like nothing has was happening. The main thing you gain from this experience is that you are unable to recall what happened during the entire day , or after a couple of days.

Feeling that you have passed through objects

There are instances when it may be that you feel like you've passed by some objects, or that you feel you are being lifted. It may be like you've been taken away from your vehicle to an entirely different vessel and being taken to an unknown location even though you're in your car. Don't think of this as an accident as it could be an alien communicating an alert that they are in your car when you are driving. In any of these situations, it is important to not ignore the obvious, but instead have a responsibility to prepare yourself to deal to the circumstance in the event of. There are times when you feel that you're trying to keep your vehicle in a specific direction but at the same you feel that a force is pulling you in the opposite direction. Many people who've felt this way are left wondering why the car is moving which they are unable to see.

2 Signs of Alien Abduction In The Day

Aliens aren't as accustomed to revealing their presence just at night or when you're busy with something. In fact , there are reports that they appear in the daytime or are doing something that you see , but it is difficult to give an explanation that is rational to the event. If you've experienced something odd in the course of the day, you should not just ignore the incident, but try to discover the reason why it transpired and the reason for it. It is believed that the alien said to be discovered in Brazil didn't appear at the mid-night, however, it was seen during the day at a very early time in the morning, to be precise.

If you're trying to find different ways that you can determine whether an alien's involvement in an event that occurs in the course of the day, then you must pay some focus to the specifics that occur and find it difficult to explain and account for. Maybe you are preparing for a homecoming ceremony of an alien within your family and the other aliens. A few of the things you must look to observe during the entire procedure are as follows.

Unnatural natural phenomena

There are times when you can observe certain natural phenomena occurring at an unusual time of day with no having prior notice. For instance , you might notice the smoke that appears out of the blue. You might be tempted to look into what's happening, but you are unable to find a specific explanation for the reason. Sometimes , you will see the formation of a dense fog one at a time that it's unnatural for it to occur, or even to form fogs. For a normal human, you might think that this would be normal, however, these kinds of instances are not natural.

The feeling of spotting an unknown in a certain direction

There are some who feel they are suffering from an overwhelming fear of walking to a specific location where they are hoping to find something they don't have any idea of. The majority of them decide to drive in the exact location with the expectation that they will find something that is drawing them to that particular spot. What attracts them is familiar, yet they are unable to identify the difference between what they are seeing and. Also, at this point there is a strong feeling of fear that is enough to cause them to go in this particular direction. You feel as if you'll find something, but there's nothing to go for, just the normal types. There are indications that aliens are in complete control over the human mind, influencing their minds as they please or might be the person who is who is feeling this way is part of an alien race. You cannot know for certain what's happening, however you can be aware that you feel the urge to take action, but you don't know the results of, nor do you have any idea of the results of this encounter.

Physical Changes following an Alien Abduction

Physical sciences show us that there isn't an action that is not followed by a reaction. If you think that alien abductions result in nothing significant, you're mistaken. Even if you don't observe their presence doesn't necessarily mean you can't be aware of or feel the impact. The effects can be psychological or physical depending on the intensity of the individual as well as the specific impact it has on the behaviour of the individual affected. The physical changes you have to be aware of and recognize that they are from aliens include:

If you begin to notice nose bleeding and you have no rational explanation then you must know that there was an encounter with an alien or that the alien was able to steal you without knowing.

If you feel a weird sensation of stiffness in one area of your body. There are some who have noticed that a portion of their skin has been cut off. It is possible that the alien had taken a samples for them to perform some research in their world. If you notice an itch on your body, it could be another reason to determine the reason for it and however, you're in good health.

Conclusion

How to determine if you've been abducted and learn the tales of the People Who Have The plethora of questions you were asking about alien abductions might be less. It's possible that there's no more.

If you take the discussion included in this book as a reference Have you done so?

As you can see that, despite the fact that there could be a myriad of reports of abductions, studies and proof of whether aliens exist, a lot of people are skeptical about the issue. The mystery of non-human creatures persists. But, as you know the nature of alien abductions according to various sources, abduction signs and what an typical abduction claim is of, and the tales of those who were abducted, you're ahead of the curve.

Thank you for your kind words and good luck!